TEACHER'S PET PUBLICATIONS

LITPLAN TEACHER PACK
for
Number the Stars
based on the book by
Lois Lowry

Written by
Janine H. Sherman

© 1996 Teacher's Pet Publications
All Rights Reserved

This **LitPlan** for Lois Lowry's
Number the Stars
has been brought to you by Teacher's Pet Publications, Inc.

Copyright Teacher's Pet Publications 1996
11504 Hammock Point
Berlin MD 21811

Only the student materials in this unit plan (such as worksheets, study questions, and tests) may be reproduced multiple times for use in the purchaser's classroom.

For any additional copyright questions,
contact Teacher's Pet Publications.

www.tpet.com

TABLE OF CONTENTS - *Number the Stars*

Introduction	5
Unit Objectives	8
Reading Assignment Sheet	9
Unit Outline	10
Study Questions (Short Answer)	13
Quiz/Study Questions (Multiple Choice)	25
Pre-reading Vocabulary Worksheets	45
Lesson One (Introductory Lesson)	63
Nonfiction Assignment Sheet	65
Oral Reading Evaluation Form	75
Writing Assignment 1	64
Writing Assignment 2	73
Writing Assignment 3	82
Writing Evaluation Form	71
Vocabulary Review Activitie	92
Extra Writing Assignments/Discussion ?s	86
Unit Review Activities	94
Unit Tests	97
Unit Resource Materials	131
Vocabulary Resource Materials	147

A FEW NOTES ABOUT THE AUTHOR
Lois Lowry

LOWRY, Lois (1937-   ). Lois Lowry is the author of over twenty juvenile novels, and has contributed stories, articles, and photographs to many leading periodicals. Her literary awards are numerous and extensive. She once said that she gauges her success as a writer by her ability to "help adolescents answer their own questions about life, identify and human relationships."

Lois Lowry was born in Honolulu, Hawaii. At the time of her birth, Lowry's father, a career army officer, was stationed near Pearl Harbor. The family separated with the onset of World War II, and Lowry spent the duration of the war with her mother's family in the Amish country of Pennsylvania. Much later, Lowry's wartime experience inspired her fourth novel, *Autumn Street*. As an author, she has often translated her life into fiction for the purpose of helping others who may have suffered under similar
circumstances.

Memories of her childhood, as well as her experiences as a parent, have led Lowry to her most popular character: *Anatasia Krupnik*, the spunky, rebellious, and irreverent adolescent who stars in a series of books that began in 1979. The broad audience appeal of the first Anatasia book prompted Lowry to write another novel featuring her heroine. "I have the feeling she's going to go on forever-or until I get sick of her, which hasn't' happened yet." Subsequent Anatasia titles number nine at the current time.

In 1990 Lowry received her highest honors. She was awarded the Newbery Medal, National Jewish Book Award, and Sidney Taylor, National Jewish Libraries, all for her World War II tale of Nazi-occupied Denmark, *Number the Stars*. In this novel she is able to create suspense and tension without wavering from the viewpoint of Annemarie, a child who shows the true meaning of courage. Based on a factual account, the inspiration for this novel came from the stories told to Lowry by a friend who was herself, a child in Copenhagen during the long years of the German occupation.

With so many accomplishments in the field of children's literature to her credit, Lowry reflects on her career in the following manner. "When I write, I draw a great deal from my own past. There is a satisfying sense of continuity, for me, in the realization that my own experiences, fictionalized, touch young readers in subtle and very personal ways." Ms. Lowry divides her time between Boston and New Hampshire.

INTRODUCTION

This unit has been designed to develop students' reading, writing, thinking, and language skills through exercises and activities related to *Number the Stars* by Lois Lowry. It includes seventeen lessons, supported by extra resource materials.

The **introductory lesson** introduces students to background information about places, people, and events mentioned throughout this novel. It also doubles as the first writing assignment for the unit. Following the introductory activity, students are given an explanation of how the activity relates to the book they are about to read. Following the transition, students are given the materials they will be using during the unit.

The **reading assignments** are approximately twenty pages each; some are a little shorter while others are a little longer. Students have approximately 15 minutes of Pre-reading work to do prior to each reading assignment. This Pre-reading work involves reviewing the study questions for the assignment and doing some vocabulary work for 10 to 12 vocabulary words they will encounter in their reading.

The **study guide questions** are fact-based questions; students can find the answers to these questions right in the text. These questions come in two formats: short answer or multiple choice. The best use of these materials is probably to use the short answer version of the questions as study guides for students (since answers will be more complete), and to use the multiple choice version for occasional quizzes. It might be a good idea to make transparencies of your answer keys for the overhead projector.

The **vocabulary work** is intended to enrich students' vocabularies as well as to aid in the students' understanding of the book. Prior to each reading assignment, students will complete a two-part worksheet for approximately 10 to 12 vocabulary words in the upcoming reading assignment. Part I focuses on students' use of general knowledge and contextual clues by giving the sentence in which the word appears in the text. Students are then to write down what they think the words mean based on the words' usage. Part II nails down the definitions of the words by giving students dictionary definitions of the words and having students match the words to the correct definitions based on the words' contextual usage. Students should then have an understanding of the words when they meet them in the text.

After each reading assignment, students will go back and formulate answers for the study guide questions. Discussion of these questions serves as a **review** of the most important events and ideas presented in the reading assignments.

After students complete extra discussion questions, there is a **vocabulary review** lesson which pulls together all of the fragmented vocabulary lists for the reading assignments and gives students a review of all of the words they have studied.

Following the reading of the book, two lessons are devoted to the **extra discussion questions/writing assignments/activities**. These questions focus on interpretation, critical analysis and personal response, employing a variety of thinking skills and adding to the students' understanding of the novel. These questions are done as a **group activity**. Using the information they have acquired so far through individual work and class discussions, students get together to further examine the text and to brainstorm ideas relating to the themes of the novel.

The group activity is followed by a **reports and discussion/ activity** session in which the groups share their ideas about the book with the entire class; thus, the entire class gets exposed to many different ideas regarding the themes and events of the book.

There are three **writing assignments** in this unit, each with the purpose of informing, persuading, or having students express personal opinions. The first assignment is to inform: students write a composition about one of the background topics assigned in Lesson One. The second assignment is to give students the opportunity to express personal ideas: students will write an account of the first time they visited the sea (or some other impressive geographical site). The third assignment gives students the chance to persuade: students will pretend to be Annemarie Johansen when she was approached by the Nazi soldiers on her way to deliver an important package to her uncle. Their objective is to convince the soldiers to allow her go her merry way without drawing attention to the package.

The **nonfiction reading assignment** is tied in with Writing Assignment 1 and the introductory lesson. Students are required to read a piece of nonfiction related in some way to *Number the Stars*. In this case, the topics are assigned in Lesson One. After reading their nonfiction pieces, students will fill out a worksheet on which they answer questions regarding facts, interpretation, criticism, and personal opinions. During one class period, students make **oral presentations** about the nonfiction pieces they have read. This not only exposes all students to a wealth of information, it also gives students the opportunity to practice **public speaking**.

The **review lesson** pulls together all of the aspects of the unit. The teacher is given four or five choices of activities or games to use which all serve the same basic function of reviewing all of the information presented in the unit.

The **unit test** comes in two formats: all multiple choice-matching-true/false or with a mixture of matching, short answer, and composition. As a convenience, two different tests for each format have been included.

There are additional **support materials** included with this unit. The **extra activities section** includes suggestions for an in-class library, crossword and word search puzzles related to the novel, and extra vocabulary worksheets. There is a list of **bulletin board ideas** which gives the teacher suggestions for bulletin boards to go along with this unit. In addition, there is a list of **extra class activities** the teacher could choose from to enhance the unit or as a substitution for an exercise the teacher might feel is inappropriate for his/her class. **Answer keys** are located directly after the **reproducible student materials** throughout the unit. The student materials may be reproduced for use in the teacher's classroom without infringement of copyrights. No other portion of this unit may be reproduced without the written consent of Teacher's Pet Publications, Inc.

UNIT OBJECTIVES - *Number the Stars*

1. Through reading Lois Lowry's *Number the Stars*, students will gain understanding of the importance of loyalty and courage, despite existing adversity.

2. Students will demonstrate their understanding of the text on four levels: factual, interpretive, critical and personal.

3. Students will do background research to become familiar with and gain meaning from life in Europe during World War II, focusing on the Jewish plight in Europe.

4. Students will define their own viewpoints on the aforementioned themes.

5. Students will gain appreciation for and demonstrate proficiency in identifying and using figurative language.

6. Students will be given the opportunity to practice reading aloud and silently to improve their skills in each area.

7. Students will answer questions to demonstrate their knowledge and understanding of the main events and characters in *Number the Stars* as they relate to the author's theme development.

8. Students will enrich their vocabularies and improve their understanding of the novel through the vocabulary lessons prepared for use in conjunction with the novel.

9. The writing assignments in this unit are geared to several purposes:
    a. To have students demonstrate their abilities to inform, to persuade, or to express their own personal ideas
        Note: Students will demonstrate ability to write effectively to <u>inform</u> by developing and organizing facts to convey information. Students will demonstrate the ability to write effectively to <u>persuade</u> by selecting and organizing relevant information, establishing an argumentative purpose, and by designing an appropriate strategy for an identified audience. Students will demonstrate the ability to write effectively to <u>express personal ideas</u> by selecting a form and its appropriate elements.
    b. To check the students' reading comprehension
    c. To make students think about the ideas presented by the novel
    d. To encourage logical thinking
    e. To provide an opportunity to practice good grammar and improve students' use of the English language.

READING ASSIGNMENT SHEET - *Number the Stars*

Date Assigned	Reading Assignment (Chapters)	Completion Date
	1, 2	
	3, 4	
	5, 6	
	7, 8	
	9, 10, 11	
	12, 13, 14, 15	
	16, 17, Afterword	

UNIT OUTLINE - *Number the Stars*

1 Library Writing Assignment #1	2 Introduction PVR Ch 1,2	3 Study? Ch. 1, 2 PVR Ch. 3,4	4 Study? Ch. 3, 4 PVR Ch. 5,6	5 Study ? Ch. 5,6 Writing Conference PVR Ch. 7, 8
6 Study ? Ch. 7, 8 Writing Assignment #2	7 PV Ch. 9,10,11 Read Ch. 9- 11	8 Group Activity Figurative Language	9 Study ? Ch. 9, 10,11 PVR Ch. 12-15	10 Study ? Ch. 12-15 Writing Assignment #3
11 PVR Ch. 16,17 PV Afterword	12 Read Afterword Study ? Ch. 16, 17& Afterword	13 Extra Discussion Questions	14 Extra Discussion Questions	15 Vocabulary Review
16 Review	17 Test	18	19	20

Key: P = Preview Study Questions   V = Vocabulary Work   R = Read

STUDY GUIDE QUESTIONS

SHORT ANSWER STUDY GUIDE QUESTIONS - *Number the Stars*

Chapters 1, 2
1. Describe Annemarie Johansen.
2. Who is Ellen Rosen?
3. Why do the Nazi soldiers stop the girls on Osterbrogade?
4. Who is Kirsti?
5. Give the setting for this novel.
6. What were the girls' mothers drinking instead of coffee?
7. Explain what is meant by Nazi occupation.
8. What is the Resistance?
9. How did Resistance members operate?
10. What does Kirsti beg to be told?
11. What significance is there to being greeted by a king?
12. Name King Christian X's bodyguard.
13. Why did King Christian X surrender to the Nazis rather than fight them?
14. What nearby country to Denmark remained neutral?
15. Why didn't Lise marry her fiance Peter?
16. According to Annemarie, the whole world had changed, except one thing. What?

Chapters 3, 4
1. Why did the Rosens install a stove in their chimney?
2. Mr. Rosen was frustrated while grading his school papers at night. Why?
3. What discovery did the girls make when they stopped at the button shop on their way home?
4. Who does Annemarie say must be the bodyguard of the Jews?
5. Describe Peter.
6. Why is it frightening to Kirsti for Peter to visit them late at night?
7. For what was Annemarie glad as she snuggled herself back in bed after Peter's visit?
8. What caused Kirsti to be so upset upon her and Mama's return from shopping?
9. How does Ellen offer to solve this problem?
10. Kirsti was told there was a firework display for her birthday. What really happened?
11. What causes the Rosens to change their plans to celebrate the Jewish New Year?
12. What is meant by the term 'relocation'?
13. In what ways do the Johansens help the Rosens that day?

Short Answer Study Guide Questions - *Number the Stars* Page 2

Chapters 5, 6
1. What does Ellen want to be when she grows up?
2. How does Ellen verbally express the sadness she felt when Annemarie's sister Lise died?
3. Where are Lise's things packed away?
4. Who awakened the Johansens late that night?
5. For what reason had they come?
6. What does Annemarie yank from Ellen and why?
7. Compare these soldiers to the ones who stopped the girls on the street.
8. In what way does the soldier insult Mama?
9. Why did Papa tear the photographs from the family album to show the soldiers?
10. How does the officer treat the baby photograph of Lise?
11. After the soldiers left, Annemarie realized she had an imprint of what in her clenched hand?
12. Mama and Papa speak of Lise that night. How long had it been since they had done so?
13. Why does Mrs. Johansen think her husband should stay home from the trip to her brother's?
14. When her father calls Uncle Henrik, he uses two phrases that confuse Annemarie. Name them.
15. Annemarie is nervous and afraid when the soldiers on the train listen to the chatter of her younger sister, Kirsti. What is she afraid Kirsti will say?
16. Once they arrive in Gilleleje and debark from the train, instead of taking the road, how do Mama and the girls reach Uncle Henrick's house? How far is it?

Chapters 7, 8
1. Describe Uncle Henrik's house.
2. While looking at the sea, what information does Ellen share with Annemarie about her mother?
3. Name the country Annemarie and Ellen can see from the seashore.
4. In what way does Mama warn the girls when they return from looking at the sea?
5. Compare the girls' usual breakfast in Copenhagen to their breakfast at Uncle Henrick's.
6. What rationed item does Annemarie joke about?
7. How does Mama spend the day?
8. Annemarie hears Mama and her uncle use two familiar, yet unknown phrases again. What are they? What does she think they refer to?
9. The girls are told about an event that will take place there that night. What is it?
10. Why is Annemarie angry and confused?

Short Answer Study Guide Questions - *Number the Stars* Page 3

Chapters 9, 10, 11
1. Uncle Henrik admits that he and Mama lied to Annemarie. What reason does he give her?
2. Now that Annemarie knows some of the truth, why doesn't she tell Ellen?
3. Other than Peter, what familiar couple is among the people that arrive for the funeral at Uncle Henrik's that night?
4. In what manner does Mama answer the Nazi soldier when he questions why the casket is not open?
5. When Mama offers to open the coffin, what does the Nazi do?
6. What is Annemarie thinking while Peter reads the psalm aloud?
7. Tell what is really in the casket.
8. What does Peter do to the baby in the group?
9. Peter gives something to Mr. Rosen. What are his instructions?
10. What does Peter do that shows Annemarie that he is now an adult, like her mother or father?
11. Stripped of all their possessions and deeds, what quality does Annemarie still recognize in the Jews as they depart for the boat?

Chapters 12, 13, 14, 15
1. On what did Mr. Rosen trip outside Henrik's house?
2. How long did Annemarie calculate it would take for her mother to return from taking the Rosens down the path to the harbor?
3. What has happened to hasten her mother's return?
4. While examining her mother's ankle at the foot of the steps, what does Annemarie find?
5. Annemarie must now take a basket with what is in it to the boat in the harbor?
6. What story does Annemarie tell herself while she is traveling on the path?
7. Who does Annemarie will herself to act like when the soldiers stop her on the path?
8. How do the soldiers treat the lunch in the basket?
9. What do the soldiers do with the packet that is in the bottom of the basket?
10. When Annemarie finally reaches the harbor to give her uncle the basket, why is she puzzled?

Chapters 16, 17, Afterword
1. Upon her return to Uncle Henrik's house, what did Annemarie have to do for the first time?
2. Tell how Uncle Henrik explains 'brave' to Annemarie.
3. How did the fishermen smuggle the Jews out of Denmark to Sweden?
4. Explain the significance of the handkerchief.
5. How does Uncle Henrik say Annemarie helped the Jews?
6. How many more years did the war last?
7. What happened to Peter?
8. What was the truth about Lise's death?
9. Annemarie goes to Lise's trunk and retrieves something that is broken. What is it and what does she ask her father?
10. Is this a true story?
11. What parts of this story are historically accurate?
12. What does Peter wish for his country in his deathbed letter?

STUDY GUIDE QUESTIONS - *Number the Stars*

Chapters 1, 2

1. Describe Annemarie Johansen.
   She is a lanky, silver-haired, ten-year-old Danish girl who is an avid runner.

2. Who is Ellen Rosen?
   She is Annemarie's neighbor and best friend. She has dark hair, which she wears in pigtails, and is stocky. She is Jewish and a good student.

3. Why do the Nazi soldiers stop the girls on Osterbrogade?
   They are racing down the street. The soldiers say they look like hoodlums when they run.

4. Who is Kirsti?
   She is Annemarie's obstinate five-year-old sister.

5. Give the setting for this novel.
   The setting is in Copenhagen, Denmark during World War II.

6. What were the girls' mothers drinking instead of coffee?
   They were sipping hot water flavored with herbs because there was no real coffee or tea during the shortages caused by the war.

7. Explain what is meant by Nazi occupation.
   This is when the Nazis take over their country.

8. What is the Resistance?
   The Resistance consists of people in Denmark who secretly are determined to do harm to the Nazis in any way possible.

9. How did Resistance members operate?
   They damaged the Nazis' cars and trucks, bombed their factories, even damaged railroad lines.

10. What does Kirsti beg to be told?
    She begs to be told a fairy tale before bed.

11. What significance is there to being greeted by a king?
    Annemarie's older sister Lise told her that it means you are special forever.

12. Name King Christian X's bodyguard.
    All of Denmark is his bodyguard.

13. Why did King Christian X surrender to the Nazis rather than fight them?
    He knew how few soldiers Denmark had. He knew that many, many Danish people would have died if they had fought.

14. What nearby country to Denmark remained neutral?
    Sweden remained neutral. There was no Nazi occupation there.

15. Why didn't Lise marry her fiance Peter?
    Annemarie's tall, beautiful, older sister had died in an accident two weeks before her wedding day.

16. According to Annemarie, the whole world had changed, except for one thing. What?
    The whole world had changed, only the fairy tales remained the same.

Chapters 3, 4

1. Why did the Rosens install a stove in their chimney?
   There was no fuel for heat, so they used the stove for heat when they could find some coal.

2. Mr. Rosen, a school teacher, was frustrated while grading his school papers at night. Why?
   Electricity was rationed, so he had to grade his papers by dim candlelight.

3. What discovery did the girls make when they stopped at the button shop on their way home?
   They found the store was closed. There was a padlock on the door as well as a German sign with a swastika on it.

4. Who does Annemarie say must be the bodyguard of the Jews?
   She thinks that all of Denmark must be the bodyguard for the Jews.

5. Describe Peter.
   Peter is Annemarie's dead sister Lise's, fiance. He has red hair and is like a son to the Johansens. He has changed from the fun-loving boy engaged to her sister to a more serious young man.

6. Why was it frightening to Kirsti for Peter to visit them late at night?
   Copenhagen had a curfew, and he was out beyond it. It was dangerous for him.

7. For what was Annemarie glad as she snuggled herself back in bed after Peter's visit?
   It was only in fairy tales that people were called to be brave. She felt that as an ordinary person, she would never be called upon for such courage.

8. What caused Kirsti to be so upset upon her and Mama's return from shopping?
    The only shoes Mama could find for Kirsti's growing feet were made out of fish skin because there was no leather available. They are green, and Kirsti despised them.

9. How did Ellen offer to solve this problem?
    She says her father has a jar of black, black ink and he could color them for her.

10. Kirsti was told there was a firework display for her August, 1943 birthday. What really happened?
    The Danes had destroyed their own naval fleet, blowing up the vessels one by one, as the Germans approached to take over the ships for their own use.

11. What caused the Rosens to change their plans to celebrate the Jewish New Year?
    That morning at the synagogue, the rabbi told his congregation that the Nazis had taken the synagogue's list of Jews. It contained all the Jews' names and addresses. The Rosens names were among them. The Nazis planned to arrest the Jews, perhaps on that night.

12. What is meant by the term 'relocation'?
    The Nazis arrest the Jews and take them away from their homes.

13. In what ways do the Johansens help the Rosens that day?
    They take Ellen, to pose as their third daughter, Lise. Peter takes Mr. and Mrs. Rosen away to someplace safe.

Chapters 5, 6

1. What does Ellen want to be when she grows up?
    Although her father wants her to become a teacher, she would like to be an actress.

2. How does Ellen verbally express the sadness she felt when Annemarie's sister Lise died?
    It was still raining the next morning when Mama told me. Mama was crying, and the rain made it seem as though the whole world was crying.

3. Where are Lise's things packed away?
    They are in a blue trunk in a corner of the bedroom.

4. Who awakened the Johansens late that night?
    Nazi soldiers came pounding on their door.

5. For what reason had they come?
    They are looking for the Rosens, who are not in their apartment.

6. What does Annemarie yank from Ellen and why?
    When Annemarie hears the Nazi soldiers, she tells Ellen to take off her Star of David necklace. Ellen can't remove it, so Annemarie yanks it off, breaking the chain.

7. Compare these soldiers to the ones who stopped the girls on the street.
    The soldiers on the street were often young and ill at ease, even smiling. These three were older and angry.

8. In what way does the soldier insult Mama?
    Noticing that her other two daughters have blond hair, he asks where did she get the dark-haired one, "From a different father, From the milkman?"

9. Why did Papa tear the photographs from the family album to show the soldiers?
    Papa tore them from the album because at the bottom of each page, below the photograph itself, was written the date. and the real Lise had been born twenty-one years earlier.

10. How does the officer treat the baby photograph of Lise?
    He tore it in half and dropped the pieces on the floor. Then he turned, the heels of his boots grinding into the picture.

11. After the soldiers left, Annemarie realized she had an imprint of what in her clenched hand?
    Annemarie relaxed the clenched fingers of her right hand , where she saw she had imprinted the Star of David into her palm.

12. Mama and Papa speak of Lise that night. How long had it been since they had done so?
    It had been three years.

13. Why does Mrs. Johansen think her husband should stay home from the trip to her brother's?
    It will appear too suspicious if he does not show up at work. They will not suspect a woman and her children.

14. When her father calls Uncle Henrik, he uses two phrases that confuse Annemarie. Name them.
    'Is the weather good for fishing?' and 'She will be bringing you a carton of cigarettes'.

15. Annemarie is nervous and afraid when the soldiers on the train listen to the chatter of her younger sister, Kirsti. What is she afraid Kirsti will say?
    She is afraid Kirsti will share that it was Ellen's New Year.

16. Once they arrive in Gilleleje and debark from the train, instead of taking the road, how do Mama and the girls reach Uncle Henrik's house? How far is it?
    It was a nice day so they took the path through the woods because it was prettier. It was close to two miles to his house.

Chapters 7, 8

1. Describe Uncle Henrik's house.
    It was an old little red-roofed farmhouse with a crooked chimney and small, shuttered windows. There was a bird's nest above a bedroom window, and a nearby apple tree was speckled with a few long ripe apples. It was surrounded by wild-flowered meadows.

2. While looking at the sea, what information does Ellen share with Annemarie about her mother?
    Her mother is afraid of the sea. It is too big and too cold for her.

3. Name the country Annemarie and Ellen can see from the seashore.
    They can see a hazy strip of land that is Sweden.

4. In what way does Mama warn the girls when they return from looking at the sea?
    She is worried they may have seen someone and warns them they must stay away from people while they are there.

5. Compare the girls' usual breakfast in Copenhagen to their breakfast at Uncle Henrik's.
    At home they have tea and bread every morning; here they have oatmeal with cream and butter.

6. What rationed item does Annemarie joke about?
    Butter. She says, "Don't tell me the soldiers try to, what's the word- relocate- butter, too?" Then Mama says, "They relocate it right into the stomach of their army!"

7. How does Mama spend the day?
    She cleans and polishes up the house, airing the rugs and washing the windows.

8. Annemarie hears Mama and her uncle use two familiar, yet unknown phrases again. What are they?
    'Tomorrow will be a day for fishing' and 'The weather is right?'

9. The girls are told about an event that will take place there that night. What is it?
    They are told there has been a death. Great Aunt Birte died and she will be resting in the house tonight, before her burial the next day.

10. Why is Annemarie angry and confused?
    She is quite certain her mother and her uncle are lying, there was no Great Aunt Birte.

Chapters 9, 10, 11
1. Uncle Henrik admits that he and Mama lied to Annemarie. What reason does he give her?
    He claims it is easier to be brave if you do not know everything. They lied to her to help her to be brave because they love her.

2. Now that Annemarie knows some of the truth, why doesn't she tell Ellen?
    She knew that she had to protect Ellen the way her mother and uncle had protected her.

3. Other than Peter, what familiar couple is among the people that arrive for the funeral at Uncle Henrik's that night?
    Ellen's parents, Mr. and Mrs. Rosen come for the funeral.

4. In what manner does Mama answer the Nazi soldier when he questions why the casket is not open?
    She tells him that the doctor said it should be closed, because she died of typhus and there was a chance the germs would still be there.

5. When Mama offers to open the coffin, what does the Nazi do?
    He slapped her and told her to open it after they leave.

6. What is Annemarie thinking while Peter reads the psalm aloud?
    When he reads the part about 'he who numbers the stars', she wonders how could anybody number them one by one, the sky is too big, there were too many. She remembers Ellen's mother thinking the sea was too big and too cold. She thinks the whole world is too big, too cold, and too cruel.

7. Tell what is really in the casket.
    There are folded clothes and blankets in the casket.

8. What does Peter do to the baby in the group?
    He asks the mother how much she weighs, and gives her the correct dosage of some liquid to make her sleep.

9. Peter gives something to Mr. Rosen. What are his instructions?
    He hands him a packet that is of great importance. He tells him to deliver it without fail, to Henrik, because he might not see him.

10. What does Peter do that shows Annemarie that he is now an adult, like her mother or father?
    He calls Annemarie's mother by her name, Inge, instead of Mrs. Johansen or Mama.

11. Stripped of all their possessions and deeds, what quality does Annemarie still recognize in the Jews as they depart for the boat?
    She sees pride in their straight shoulders as they start down the dark path.

Chapters 12, 13, 14, 15
1. On what did Mr. Rosen trip outside Henrik's house?
    He tripped on the loose step outside the kitchen door.

2. How long did Annemarie calculate it would take for her mother to return from taking the Rosens down the path to the harbor?
    She figures her mother will be back by three-thirty in the morning. This is one hour from when she left.

3. What has happened to hasten her mother's return?
    She tripped over a root in the path and went sprawling.

4. While examining her mother's ankle at the foot of the steps, what does Annemarie find?
    She finds the packet Peter had given Mr. Rosen in the grass. He must have dropped it when he tripped on the step.

5. Annemarie must now take a basket with what in it to the boat in the harbor?
    She must take a basket with bread, an apple and some cheese in it, with the packet hidden underneath. It will look like her uncle's forgotten lunch.

6. What story does Annemarie tell herself while she is traveling on the path?
    She tells herself a story she often tells Kirsti, *Little Red Riding Hood*.

7. Who does Annemarie will herself to act like when the soldiers stop her on the path?
    She wills herself, with all her being, to behave as Kirsti would.

8. How do the soldiers treat the lunch in the basket?
    They tear up the bread, play with the cheese, and throw the apple on the ground.

9. What do the soldiers do with the packet that is in the bottom of the basket?
    They tear it open and make fun of the handkerchief within. They throw it to the ground to join the apple.

10. When Annemarie finally reaches the harbor to give her uncle the basket, why is she puzzled?
    She thought she would see the Jewish people on the boat Uncle Henrik was taking to Sweden.

Chapters 16, 17, Afterword
1. Upon her return to Uncle Henrik's house, what did Annemarie have to do for the first time?
    Blossom, the cow needed milked, so she milked her.

2. Tell how Uncle Henrik explains 'brave' to Annemarie.
   When she claims she was not brave, but frightened, he tells her that brave means- not thinking about the dangers, just thinking about what you must do.

3. How did the fishermen smuggle the Jews out of Denmark to Sweden?
   The Jews come to the coast and the fishermen hide them in carefully concealed places on their boats, often throwing fish on top of the decks

4. Explain the significance of the handkerchief.
   The handkerchief contains a special drug that attracts the dogs, but when they sniff at it, it ruins their sense of smell. When the dogs show up at the harbor and start sniffing, the fishermen pull out their handkerchiefs.

5. How does Uncle Henrik say Annemarie helped the Jews?
   He says she risked her life. Without the packet, the Jews could have been discovered and harmed by the Nazis who boarded the boat.

6. How many more years did the war last?
   The war lasted another two years.

7. What happened to Peter?
   He had been captured and executed by the Germans in the public square in Copenhagen because of his involvement in the Resistance.

8. What was the truth about Lise's death?
   She and Peter were attending a Resistance meeting in a basement when it was raided by the Nazis. Running, she was run down in a car by the Nazis and killed.

9. Annemarie goes to Lise's trunk and retrieves something that is broken. What is it and what does she ask her father?
   She pulls out the broken chain of the Star of David necklace she tore from Ellen's neck that night two years ago. She asks him if he can fix it.

10. Is this a true story?
    It is based on many true facts, although the exact characters and plot are fictional.

11. What parts of this story are historically accurate?
    The following events are historically correct: Denmark surrenders to Germany, the Nazi occupation of Denmark lasted five years, Denmark's beloved King Christian rode Jubilee, unguarded, each morning, a young boy really did say that all of Denmark was his bodyguard, the Danes really sunk their own navy, New Year of 1943 the rabbis did tell their synagogue congregations of the Germans' plans, and almost the entire Jewish population was smuggled across the sea to Sweden. The handkerchief is real too. It contained rabbit's blood to attract the dogs and cocaine to then numb their sense of smell. The locations in Copenhagen and Denmark are real, as well.

12. The author fashioned the character Peter from a courageous young man she met during her research. What does this young man wish for his country in his deathbed letter?
    He wishes for his country the gift of human decency.

MULTIPLE CHOICE STUDY GUIDE/QUIZ QUESTIONS - *Number the Stars*

<u>Chapters 1, 2</u>
1. Annemarie Johansen is
    a. dark-haired
    b. twelve years old
    c. silver-haired and lanky
    d. an avid reader

2. Ellen Rosen is
    a. a dark-haired Jewish girl
    b. a blond Danish girl
    c. a good runner
    d. a Swedish girl

3. The Nazis stop the girls on the street because
    a. they stole an apple and ran
    b. they stop all the kids to harass them
    c. they are running down the street
    d. they are late for school

4. Kirsti is
    a. Mama's aunt
    b. Annemarie's younger sister
    c. Peter's wife
    d. Ellen's younger sister

5. This story takes place in
    a. Germany
    b. Switzerland
    c. Norway
    d. Copenhagen, Denmark

6. Instead of coffee the mothers drink
    a. tea
    b. orange juice
    c. herb flavored hot water
    d. hot cocoa

7. Nazi occupation is
    a. when the Germans offered jobs
    b. when the Nazis took over the country
    c. when Hitler occupied Germany
    d. when Sweden surrendered

Study Guide/Quiz Questions - Number The Stars Multiple Choice Format Page 2

8. The Resistance is
    a. a secret group against the Nazis
    b. the prevention of harm
    c. a Nazi sect
    d. an anti-Jewish sect

9. Members of the Resistance
    a. blew up ships
    b. bombed railroads
    c. smuggled Jews out
    d. all of the above

10. Kirsti begs to be told
    a. a fairy tale
    b. a nursery rhyme
    c. she is allowed to stay up late
    d. she may have a kitten

11. When a king greets you, according to Lise, you
    a. are granted privileges
    b. are special forever
    c. become his bodyguard
    d. get to go the castle

12. King Christian X's bodyguard is
    a. his son
    b. the men of Copenhagen
    c. all of Denmark
    d. a fierce warrior

13. King Christian X surrendered to Hitler because
    a. he knew too many Danish lives would be lost.
    b. Hitler threatened him.
    c. he was too old to fight.
    d. he thought it was too much work.

14. Which nearby country to Denmark remained neutral?
    a. Norway
    b. Austria
    c. Sweden
    d. Germany

Study Guide/Quiz Questions- *Number the Stars* Multiple Choice Format Page 3

15. Lise didn't marry Peter because
    a. he backed out of it.
    b. she died.
    c. she got cold feet.
    d. they agreed not to.

16. Annemarie thought the whole had changed except for
    a. the weather
    b. fairy tales
    c. King Christian
    d. her father

Study Guide/Quiz Questions- *Number the Stars* Multiple Choice Format Page 4

Chapters 3, 4

1. The Rosens install a stove in their chimney
   a. to cook on daily.
   b. to heat their apartment.
   c. for decoration.
   d. to store coal.

2. Mr. Rosen was frustrated grading his papers at night because
   a. the students didn't follow directions.
   b. of the dim candlelight.
   c. he couldn't read their writing.
   d. Ellen kept asking him questions.

3. On the way home from school, the girls discovered
   a. the button shop was closed.
   b. the soldiers were gone.
   c. the synagogue's glass was shattered.
   d. Kirsti was missing.

4. Annemarie thinks
   a. the soldiers should be the Jews' bodyguard.
   b. King Christian X should be the Jews' bodyguard.
   c. all of Denmark must be the Jews' bodyguard.
   d. Hitler should protect the Jews.

5. Peter is
   a. the button shop owner.
   b. the next door neighbor.
   c. a Nazi soldier.
   d. Lise's red-headed fiance.

6. It was frightening for Annemarie to see Peter late at night because
   a. she was awakened from a nightmare.
   b. he was out past the curfew.
   c. he seemed very angry and upset.
   d. he had been drinking beer.

7. Annemarie was glad as she snuggled down in bed after Peter's visit because
   a. she was sleepy.
   b. he had brought her a seashell.
   c. she was ordinary and wouldn't have to be brave.
   d. both a and b

Study Guide/Quiz Questions - *Number the Stars* Multiple Choice Format Page 5

8. After shopping, Kirsti was upset because
    a. her new shoes were made of fish scales.
    b. she wanted a cupcake and they were sold out.
    c. she didn't get anything.
    d. her new dress was too long.

9. Ellen offers to solve Kirsti's problem by
    a. hemming the dress.
    b. using her father's black ink.
    c. baking her some cupcakes.
    d. giving her some of her new things.

10. What Kirsti thought were fireworks really were
    a. thunderbolts.
    b. the Nazi soldiers practicing shooting from tanks.
    c. the Danish people blowing up their own naval fleet.
    d. her imagination.

11. The Rosens did not celebrate the Jewish New Year due to
    a. the synagogue's list being taken by the Germans.
    b. their chicken getting burnt in the stove.
    c. their relatives visiting at the last minute.
    d. the Nazis harassing them.

12. Relocation means
    a. the Jews stay with their relatives for awhile.
    b. arresting the Resistance fighters.
    c. taking the Danes to Sweden.
    d. arresting the Jews and taking them away to camps and ghettos.

13. The Johansens help the Rosens by
    a. cooking their chicken for them and saving it.
    b. hiding Ellen and helping the parents escape.
    c. giving them money.
    d. sending Ellen away to their relatives.

Study Guide/Quiz Questions- *Number the Stars* Multiple Choice Format Page 6

Chapters 5, 6

1. Ellen wants to be
    a. a teacher.
    b. an actress.
    c. a doctor.
    d. all of the above

2. How does Ellen express how she feels about Lise's death?
    a. She wishes she wouldn't have died.
    b. She felt like the whole world was crying.
    c. She felt like crying all day.
    d. She wanted to change what had happened.

3. Lise's things are packed away in
    a. a blue trunk in Annemarie's room.
    b. a box in Kirsti's room.
    c. a suitcase in her parents' room.
    d. the attic.

4. The Johansen's were awakened that night by
    a. Peter.
    b. The Rosens.
    c. Nazi soldiers.
    d. Hitler.

5. The visitors had come looking for
    a. money.
    b. Peter.
    c. the Star of David necklace.
    d. the Rosens.

6. Annemarie yanks
    a. Ellen's pigtails.
    b. her covers over her head.
    c. Ellen's Star of David necklace.
    d. Kirsti's doll from her.

7. The difference between these soldiers and the ones on the street are
    a. these are younger.
    b. these are grumpier.
    c. these are much nicer.
    d. these are older and angrier.

Study Guide/Quiz Questions- *Number the Stars* Multiple Choice Format Page 7

8. The soldiers insult Mama by
    a. criticizing her housekeeping.
    b. sneering at her needlework.
    c. tasting some food and then spitting it out.
    d. insinuating there was another father for one of her daughters.

9. Papa tore the pictures from the family album because
    a. they were getting old.
    b. he didn't want the soldiers to see the dates written underneath them.
    c. he wanted to put them in another place.
    d. he wanted to hide them from the soldiers.

10. The officer treats Lise's baby photo
    a. carefully.
    b. carelessly.
    c. gently.
    d. destructively.

11. Annemarie opened her clenched hand after the soldiers left to find
    a. an imprint of the Star of David.
    b. she burst a blood vessel.
    c. her hand was swollen.
    d. she had dropped the necklace somewhere.

12. How long had it been since Annemarie's parents had spoken of Lise?
    a. 2 months
    b. 3 months
    c. 2 years
    d. 3 years

13. Mrs. Johansen thinks her husband should stay home from the trip because
    a. he needs the money and can't miss work.
    b. she wants a little vacation away from him and the house.
    c. it will look less suspicious.
    d. the kids will get on his nerves.

14. Choose the phrase that means something other than what it states.
    a. The eggs are fried.
    b. She will bring a carton of cigarettes.
    c. Is the weather good for fishing?
    d. Both b and c

Study Guide/Quiz Questions- *Number the Stars* Multiple Choice Format Page 8

15. On the train, Annemarie is afraid that Kirsti will
    a. say that it's Ellen's New Year.
    b. tell Ellen is Jewish.
    c. annoy the soldiers.
    d. eat too much and get sick.

16. Mama and the girls go from the train stop in Gilleleje to Uncle Henrik's house by
    a. the road through town.
    b. the 2 mile path through the woods.
    c. the road outside of town.
    d. the .5 mile path near town.

Study Guide/Quiz Questions- *Number the Stars* Multiple Choice Format Page 9

Chapters 7, 8
1. Which of the following was not part of Uncle Henrik's house?
    a. bird nest
    b. blue shutters
    c. crooked chimney
    d. red roof

2. Ellen shares with Annemarie that
    a. she is afraid of the sea.
    b. her father loves the sea.
    c. she used to visit the sea every summer.
    d. her mother is afraid of the sea.

3. Annemarie and Ellen can see
    a. Sweden.
    b. Norway.
    c. Germany.
    d. Austria.

4. Mama warns the girls about
    a. the fishing village.
    b. the Nazis.
    c. talking to anyone .
    d. the dangers of the sea.

5. The girls' breakfast at Uncle Henrik's is
    a. the same thing they have in Copenhagen.
    b. much better than they have in Copenhagen.
    c. worse that their usual breakfast.
    d. later than their usual breakfast.

6. Annemarie jokes about the rationed
    a. electricity.
    b. coffee.
    c. sugar.
    d. butter.

7. Mama spends the day at her brother's
    a. cleaning and polishing.
    b. baking and cooking.
    c. visiting with him.
    d. taking the girls to the seashore.

Study Guide/Quiz Questions- *Number the Stars* Multiple Choice Format Page 10

8. Which phrase is not a code?
   a. The weather is not good for fishing.
   b. Tomorrow will be a good day for fishing.
   c. The neighbors are home.
   d. None of the above

9. That night at Uncle Henrik's there will be
   a. a funeral.
   b. a dinner.
   c. a party.
   d. a seance.

10. Annemarie is angry and confused because
    a. she is homesick.
    b. she has never heard of Great Aunt Birte.
    c. she wants to go to bed.
    d. she can't share a room with Ellen.

Study Guide/Quiz Questions- *Number the Stars* Multiple Choice Format Page 11

Chapters 9, 10, 11
1. Uncle Henrik admits he and Mama lied to Annemarie because
    a. they couldn't trust her immaturity.
    b. they wanted to protect her.
    c. they were afraid.
    d. all of the above

2. After Annemarie learns the truth, she immediately tells Ellen to lessen her fears.
    a. true
    b. false

3. Who, that is familiar, arrives at Uncle Henrik's that night besides Peter?
    a. Lise
    b. Mr. and Mrs. Rosen
    c. Nazis
    d. Thor

4. Mama tells the soldiers the casket is closed because
    a. of the cause of death.
    b. the doctor advised it.
    c. there could still be germs.
    d. all of the above

5. When Mama offers to open the coffin the soldier
    a. waits patiently.
    b. laughs.
    c. slaps Mama and says to open it later.
    d. trips her on her way to open it.

6. As Peter reads the psalm aloud, Annemarie thinks
    a. about how scared she is.
    b. and wonders how someone could number each star because of the sky's size.
    c. and wonders what will happen next.
    d. she will faint from exhaustion.

7. In the casket are
    a. clothes and blankets.
    b. dead bodies they borrowed.
    c. lanterns and candles.
    d. guns and ammunition.

Study Guide/Quiz Questions- *Number the Stars* Multiple Choice Format Page 12

8. Peter tells the mother of the baby she must keep the child silent.
    a. true
    b. false

9. Peter's instructions to Mr. Rosen include to
    a. deliver the packet to Henrik without fail.
    b. deliver the envelope to the Swedish police.
    c. take the packet to the pretend funeral.
    d. wrap the lunch up in the basket to hide the packet.

10. One way Peter shows his maturity is by
    a. issuing instructions to the adults.
    b. calling the uncle by his first name.
    c. planning the funeral.
    d. addressing Mama as Inge.

11. What quality does Annemarie see in the Jewish people as they leave?
    a. fear
    b. pride
    c. love
    d. freedom

Study Guide/Quiz Questions- *Number the Stars* Multiple Choice Format Page 13

Chapters 12, 13, 14, 15
1. Mr. Rosen tripped outside Henrik's house on
    a. the loose step.
    b. a tree root.
    c. a tree limb.
    d. the leftover leaves.

2. How long does Annemarie figure it will take her mother to return?
    a. one-half hour
    b. two hours
    c. one hour
    d. one and one-half hour

3. Mrs. Johansen has had what sort of mishap?
    a. stopped by the Nazis
    b. tripped on the loose step
    c. got confused on the path
    d. tripped on a tree root on the path

4. While helping her mother, Annemarie finds
    a. the important packet Peter gave Mr. Rosen.
    b. the baby's medicine.
    c. the Bible from which Peter read.
    d. a secret place under the step.

5. Annemarie must rush to the fishing boat to deliver
    a. her Uncle's lunch.
    b. the packet Peter gave Mr. Rosen.
    c. an envelope to the Rosens.
    d. Ellen's necklace.

6. The story Annemarie tells herself on the way to the boat is
    a. Gone With the Wind.
    b. The King and I.
    c. Hansel and Gretel.
    d. Little Red Riding Hood.

7. When the soldiers stop her, Annemarie wills herself to act like
    a. Mama.
    b. Peter.
    c. Kirsti.
    d. Ellen.

Study Guide/Quiz Questions- *Number the Stars* Multiple Choice Format Page 14

8. Choose the one word that does not describe how the soldiers treated Annemarie on the path.
    a. considerately
    b. nastily
    c. contemptibly
    d. rudely

9. What do the soldiers do with the important thing in the lunch?
    a. They blow their noses on it.
    b. They tear it open and toss on the ground.
    c. They feed it to the dogs.
    d. They eat it.

10. When Annemarie reached the harbor, what was missing?
    a. the Jewish people
    b. the handkerchief
    c. the lunch basket
    d. her uncle's boat

Study Guide/Quiz Questions- *Number the Stars* Multiple Choice Format Page 15

Chapters 16, 17, and Afterword
1. What task faced Annemarie upon her return?
       a. taking her mother to the doctor
       b. making breakfast for Mama and Kirsti
       c. picking apples for the pie
       d. milking the cow

2. Annemarie doesn't feel like she was brave because
       a. she was frightened.
       b. she didn't stand up to the Nazis.
       c. she is just an ordinary girl.
       d. she pretended to be her sister.

3. The fishermen aided the Jews by
       a. finding their relatives for them.
       b. smuggling them in their boats to Sweden.
       c. feeding and clothing them.
       d. holding funerals for their friends.

4. The handkerchief was vital because
       a. it was a family heirloom.
       b. it had blood on it.
       c. it prevented the dogs from locating the scent of the Jews.
       d. it has Henrik's initials on it.

5. Uncle Henrik admires Annemarie for
       a. milking Blossom.
       b. risking her life.
       c. taking the dark path.
       d. saving Ellen's necklace.

6. How much longer did the war last?
       a. six months
       b. three years
       c. two years
       d. one and a half years

7. What news do the Johansen's hear of Peter?
       a. He is awarded a purple heart.
       b. He married another girl from Sweden.
       c. He moved to Sweden.
       d. He was executed by the Germans.

Study Guide/Quiz Questions- *Number the Stars* Multiple Choice Format Page 16

8. Annemarie learned that her sister Lise had been
    a. killed by the Nazis.
    b. run down by a car.
    c. a member of the Resistance.
    d. all of the above

9. Out of the Lise's trunk, Annemarie retrieves
    a. her Bible.
    b. the embroidered pillow.
    c. Ellen's necklace.
    d. Lise's yellow dress.

10. Annemarie asks her father
    a. why so many people had to die.
    b. to fix the necklace.
    c. what the psalm from the Bible meant.
    d. how many others are in the Resistance.

11. This story is
    a. fiction
    b. non-fiction

12. Select the one nonfactual item from the story below.
    a. the locations in Denmark
    b. the exact characters
    c. the handkerchief
    d. King Christian X

13. The author based the character Peter on a young man who wished for
    a. peace.
    b. love.
    c. human decency.
    d. Jewish freedom.

ANSWER KEY- MULTIPLE CHOICE STUDY/QUIZ QUESTIONS
Number the Stars

Chapters 1,2
1. C   14. C
2. A   15. B
3. C   16. B
4. B
5. D
6. C
7. B
8. A
9. D
10. A
11. B
12. C
13. A

Chapters 3,4
1. B
2. B
3. A
4. C
5. D
6. B
7. C
8. A
9. B
10. C
11. A
12. D
13. B

Chapters 5,6
1. B   14. D
2. B   15. A
3. A   16. B
4. C
5. D
6. C
7. D
8. D
9. B
10. D
11. A
12. C
13. C

Chapters 7,8
1. B
2. D
3. A
4. C
5. B
6. D
7. A
8. C
9. A
10. B

Chapters 9,10,11
1. B
2. B
3. B
4. D
5. C
6. B
7. A
8. B
9. A
10. D
11. B

Chapters 12,13,14,15
1. A
2. C
3. D
4. A
5. B
6. D
7. C
8. A
9. B
10. A

Chapters 16,17& Afterword
1. D   11. A
2. A   12. B
3. B   13. C
4. C
5. B
6. C
7. D
8. D
9. C
10. B

PREREADING VOCABULARY WORKSHEETS

VOCABULARY - *Number the Stars*

Chapters 1 and 2 Part I: Using Prior Knowledge and Contextual Clues

Below are the sentences in which the vocabulary words appear in the text. Read the sentence. Use any clues you can find in the sentence combined with your prior knowledge, and write what you think the underlined words mean on the lines provided.

1. She was a stocky ten-tear-old, unlike lanky Annemarie.

   _____

2. "Go!" shouted Annemarie, and the two girls were off, racing along the residential sidewalk.

   _____

3. Three years they've been here and still can't speak our language, Annemarie thought with contempt.

   _____

4. She reached down for Kirsti's hand, but Kirsti, always stubborn, refused it and put her hands on her hips defiantly.

   _____

5. Stand still, Kirsti, Annemarie ordered silently, praying that somehow the obstinate five-year-old would receive the message.

   _____

6. "And don't run. You look like hoodlums when you run."

   _____

7. "Are you going to tell your mother?" Ellen asked Annemarie as they trudged together up the stairs.

   _____

8. But Annemarie heard Mama and Papa talk, sometimes at night, about the news they received that way: news of sabotage against the Nazis, bombs hidden and exploded in factories that produced war materials, and industrial railroad lines damaged so that the goods couldn't be transported.

   _____

9. She glanced through the window, down to the street corner where the soldiers stood, their faces impassive beneath the metal helmets.

   _____

Vocabulary Chapters 1-2 Continued

10., 11. Mama had been <u>crocheting</u> that evening three years ago, the lacy edging of a pillowcase, part of Lise's <u>trousseau.</u>

_____

12. Her fingers moved rapidly, turning the thin white thread into an <u>intricate</u> narrow border.

_____

Part II: Determining the Meaning

Match the vocabulary words to their dictionary definitions. If there are words for which you cannot figure out the definition by contextual clues and by process of elimination, look them up in a dictionary.

___ 1. lanky
___ 2. residential
___ 3. contempt
___ 4. defiantly
___ 5. obstinate
___ 6. hoodlums
___ 7. trudged
___ 8. sabotage
___ 9. impassive
___10. trousseau
___11. crocheting
___12. intricate

A. stubborn
B. vandalize
C. lean; thin
D. unemotional; indifferent
E. detailed
F. plodded; marched
G. disgust; distaste
H. needlework similar to knitting
I. criminals; hooligans
J. items a bride brings into her marriage
K. area where homes are located
L. boldly ; rebelliously

Vocabulary - *Number the Stars* Chapters 3 and 4

Part I: Using Prior Knowledge and Contextual Clues

Below are the sentences in which the vocabulary words appear in the text. Read the sentence. Use any clues you can find in the sentence combined with your prior knowledge, and write what you think the underlined words mean on the lines provided.

1. "I did not!" Kirsti said haughtily from the bedroom doorway. "I never, ever did that!"

   _____

2. "And I suppose they took a big basket of pink frosted cupcakes with them," Annemarie said sarcastically to her sister.

   _____

3. "All right, Scarlet, I'm coming," Ellen replied in a sophisticated voice.

   _____

4. Mama followed her with an exasperated look and set a package down on the table.

   _____

5. She took the new shoes, holding them disdainfully, and put them on a chair.

   _____

6. Annemarie grinned and walked her Scarlet towards the chair that Ellen had designated as Tivoli.

   _____

7. "I did too," she said belligerently "It was my birthday. I woke up in the night and I could hear the booms. And there were lights in the sky. Mama said it was fireworks for my birthday!"

   _____

Vocabulary Chapters 3-4 Continued

8. It made Annemarie feel sad and proud, too, to picture the tall, aging king, perhaps with tears in his blue eyes, as he looked at the remains of his small navy, which now lay submerged and broken in the harbor.

_____

9. Annemarie and Kirsti had often been invited to watch Mrs. Rosen light the Sabbath candles on Fridays evenings.

_____

10. Leaving for school on Thursday with her sister, Annemarie saw the Rosens walking to the synagogue early in the morning, dressed in their best clothes.

_____

11. "About a king?" Kirsti asked dubiously. "About a king, if you wish, " Mama replied.

_____

12. "This morning, at the synagogue, the rabbi told his congregation that the Nazis have taken the synagogue lists of all he Jews.

_____

Part II: Determining the Meaning: Match the vocabulary words to their dictionary definitions.

____ 13. haughtily
____ 14. sarcastically
____ 15. sophisticated
____ 16. exasperated
____ 17. disdainfully
____ 18. designated
____ 19. belligerently
____ 20. submerged
____ 21. Sabbath
____ 22. synagogue
____ 23. dubiously
____ 24. rabbi

A. Jewish church
B. scornfully
C. arrogantly ; high and mightily
D. doubtfully
E. cultured; refined
F. in a cutting manner
G. appointed
H. Jewish minister
I. Holy day
J. plunged underwater
K. in a hostile manner
L. annoyed; irritated

Vocabulary - *Number the Stars* Chapters 5 and 6

Part I: Using Prior Knowledge and Contextual Clues

Below are the sentences in which the vocabulary words appear in the text. Read the sentence. Use any clues you can find in the sentence combined with your prior knowledge, and write what you think the underlined words mean on the lines provided.

1. Ellen stood on tiptoe again, and made an imperious gesture with her arm.

   _____

2. "I am the dark queen, " she intoned dramatically.

   _____

3. "Lise Margrett, " he read finally, and stared at Ellen for a long, unwavering moment.

   _____

4. In her mind, Annemarie pictured the photograph that he held: the baby, wide-eyed, propped against a pillow, her tiny hand holding a silver teething ring, her bare feet visible below the hem of an embroidered dress.

   _____

5. She looked down, and saw that she had imprinted the Star of David into her palm.

   _____

6. Ellen and Annemarie both smiled tentatively. For a moment their fear was eased.

   _____

7. Annemarie watched his face and knew that he was struggling with the decision. Finally he nodded, reluctantly.

   _____

8. One of them had something stuck in his teeth; he probed with his tongue and distorted his own face.

   _____

Vocabulary Chapters 5-6 Continued

9. She had been talking about Kronbourg Castle ever since they had seen it, sprawling <u>massive</u> and ancient, beside the sea, from the train.
_____

10. "Maybe they still do, but its the wrong time of year-there are just those few <u>chrysanthemums</u> left.
_____

Part II Determining the Meaning: Match the vocabulary words to their dictionary definitions.

___ 25. imperious
___ 26. intoned
___ 27. unwavering
___ 28. embroidered
___ 29. imprinted
___ 30. tentatively
___ 31. reluctantly
___ 32. distorted
___ 33. massive
___ 34. chrysanthemum

A. perennial plant
B. unwillingly; hesitant
C. decorated with needlework
D. uncertainly, unsure
E. recited; spoke
F. twisted; deformed
G. stable; steady
H. domineering, overbearing
I. huge
J. pressed into

Vocabulary - *Number the Stars* Chapters 7 and 8

Part I: Using Prior Knowledge and Contextual Clues

Below are the sentences in which the vocabulary words appear in the text. Read the sentence. Use any clues you can find in the sentence combined with your prior knowledge, and write what you think the underlined words mean on the lines provided.

1. A bird's nest, <u>wispy</u> with straw, was half hidden in the corner where the roof met the wall above a bedroom window.
   _____

2. Nearby, a <u>gnarled</u> tree was still speckled with a few apples now long past ripe.
   _____

3. At night they are all there, <u>anchored</u> in the harbor.
   _____

4. "I wish I knew where my parents are," Ellen said in a small voice as she outlined one of the <u>appliqued</u> birds with her finger.
   _____

5. The <u>Scandinavian</u> night is not very dark yet, though soon, when winter came, the night would be not only dark but very long, night skies beginning in the late afternoon and lasting through morning.
   _____

6. But it wasn't a joke at all, though Mama laughed <u>ruefully</u>.
   _____

7. Kirsti joined the laughter, as the three of them pictured a mound of frightened butter under <u>military</u> arrest.
   _____

8. Suddenly, here in the sunlit kitchen, with cream in a pitcher and a bird in the apple tree beside the door-and out in the Kattegat, where Uncle Henrik, surrounded by bright blue sky and water, pulled in his nets filled with shiny silver fish-suddenly the <u>specter</u> of guns and grim-faced soldiers seemed nothing more than a ghost story, a joke with which to frighten the children in the dark.
   _____

Vocabulary Chapters 7-8 Continued

9. "Cream," Annemarie said, <u>gesturing</u> to the pitcher with a grin.
_____

10. She remembered who had been a grouch, who had been such a <u>scold</u> that her husband had finally moved away to a different house, yet returning each evening for their meal together.

_____

Part II: Determining the Meaning   Match the vocabulary words to their dictionary definitions.

___ 35. wispy
___ 36. gnarled
___ 37. anchored
___ 38. appliqued
___ 39. Scandinavian
___ 40. ruefully
___ 41. military
___ 42. specter
___ 43. gesturing
___ 44. scold

A. vision
B. motioning
C. having to do with soldiers or army
D. referring to northern European countries
E. fabric sewn onto another decoratively
F. nag
G. secured; held fast
H. strawlike
I. knot
J. regretfully

Vocabulary - *Number the Stars* Chapters 9, 10, 11

Part I: Using Prior Knowledge and Contextual Clues

Below are the sentences in which the vocabulary words appear in the text. Read the sentence. Use any clues you can find in the sentence combined with your prior knowledge, and write what you think the underlined words mean on the lines provided.

1. He was kneeling on the straw covered floor beside the cow, his strong tan hands <u>rhythmically</u> urging the milk into the spotless bucket.

___

2. His strong hands continued, <u>deftly</u> pressing like a pulse against the cow.

___

3. He went to the window of the barn, stood in the shadows, and looked out. " It is the <u>hearse</u>, " he said. "It is Great Aunt Birte, who never was."

___

4. "So, my little friend, it is time for the night of <u>mourning</u> to begin. Are you ready?"

___

5. There was no playfulness to his affection tonight, just a sense of <u>urgency</u>, of worry.

___

6. Annemarie felt a <u>surge</u> of sadness; the bond of friendship had not broken, but it was as if Ellen had moved now into a different world, a world of her own family and whatever lay ahead for them.

___

7. She heard- as if in a recurring nightmare- the pounding on the floor, and then the heavy, frightening familiar <u>staccato</u> of boots on the kitchen floor.

___

8. "Poor Great Aunt Birte, " the soldier said, in a <u>condescending</u> voice.

___

Vocabulary Chapters 9-11 Continued

9. He relit the extinguished candle.

_____

10. After a moment of rummaging through the folded things, he found a smaller winter jacket, and handed it to Ellen.

_____

11. Annemarie could see it protruding from Mr. Rosen's pocket when he returned to the room and sat down again.

_____

12. There was a slight commotion outside the door, and Mama went quickly to look out.

_____

Part II: Determining the Meaning
    Match the vocabulary words to their dictionary definitions. If there are words for which you cannot figure out the definition by contextual clues and by process of elimination, look them up in a dictionary.

___ 45. rhythmically	A. sticking out
___ 46. deftly	B. put out
___ 47. hearse	C. superior
___ 48. mourning	D. sharp, abrupt sounds
___ 49. urgency	E. searching through
___ 50. surge	F. to a uniform beat
___ 51. staccato	G. grieving
___ 52. condescending	H. funeral vehicle
___ 53. extinguished	I. skillfully
___ 54. rummaging	J. seriousness
___ 55. protruding	K. disturbance
___ 56. commotion	L. rush

Vocabulary - *Number the Stars*-Chapters 12-15

Part I: Using Prior Knowledge and Contextual Clues

Below are the sentences in which the vocabulary words appear in the text. Read the sentence. Use any clues you can find in the sentence combined with your prior knowledge, and write what you think the underlined words mean on the lines provided.

1. She <u>winced</u> in pain.
   _____

2. Her mother didn't answer. Her face was <u>stricken</u>. She looked at the path and down at her ankle.
   _____

3. She had watched and helped, earlier, as the others <u>donned</u> sweaters, jackets, and coats.
   _____

4. The path, <u>latticed</u> with thick roots hidden under the fallen leaves, was invisible.
   _____

5. "Once upon a time there was a little girl," she told herself silently, "who had a beautiful red <u>cloak</u>."
   _____

6. Annemarie always tried to prolong this part, to build up the suspense and <u>tantalize</u> her sister.
   _____

7. With them, straining at <u>taut</u> leashes, were two large dogs, their eyes glittering, their lips curled.
   _____

8. Please, please, she <u>implored</u> in her mind. Don't lift the napkin.
   _____

9. "You know we have no meat, " she said <u>insolently</u>.
   _____

10. He gestured with the folded white cloth and gave a short, <u>caustic</u> laugh.
    _____

Vocabulary Chapters 12-15 Continued

11. The dogs lunged, sniffed at it eagerly, then subsided, disappointed again.

_____

Part II: Determining the Meaning
　　Match the vocabulary words to their dictionary definitions.

___ 57. winced
___ 58. stricken
___ 59. donned
___ 60. latticed
___ 61. cloak
___ 62. tantalize
___ 63. taut
___ 64. implored
___ 65. insolently
___ 66. caustic
___ 67. lunged
___ 68. subsided

A. Criss-crossed
B. Tease; arouse
C. Tight
D. Hit by strong emotion
E. Outer garment
F. Pleaded; begged
G. Shrunk back; flinched
H. Put on
I. Let up; eased
J. Sudden forward movement
K. Rudely; disrespectfully
L. Harsh

Vocabulary - *Number the Stars* Chapters 16, 17 & Afterword

Part I: Using Prior Knowledge and Contextual Clues

Below are the sentences in which the vocabulary words appear in the text. Read the sentence. Use any clues you can find in the sentence combined with your prior knowledge, and write what you think the underlined words mean.

1. But Annemarie forced herself to think of the red-headed almost - brother, and how <u>devastating</u> the day was when they received the news that Peter had been captured and executed by the Germans in the public square at Ryvangen, in Copenhagen.

2. Later, Annemarie had gone to the place with her parents and they had laid flowers there, on the <u>bleak</u>, numbered ground.

3. The little Star of David still <u>gleamed</u> gold.

4., 5., 6. I had always been fascinated and moved by Annelise's descriptions not only of the personal <u>deprivation</u> that her family and their neighbors suffered during those years, and the <u>sacrifices</u> they made, but even more by the greater picture she drew for me of the courage and <u>integrity</u> of the Danish people under the leadership of the King they loved so much, Christian X.

7. After the Nazis began to use police dogs to sniff out hidden passengers on the fishing boats, Swedish scientists worked swiftly to prevent such <u>detection</u>.

8. Almost every boat captain used such a <u>permeated</u> handkerchief, and many lives were saved by the device.

9. The dream for you all, young and old, must be to create an ideal of human decency, and not a narrow-minded and <u>prejudiced</u> one.

Vocabulary Chapter 16 - End Continued

Part II: Determining the Meaning
    Match the vocabulary words to their dictionary definitions. If there are words for which you cannot figure out the definition by contextual clues and by process of elimination, look them up in a dictionary.

___ 69. devastating   A. Shone; flickered
___ 70. bleak   B. Disastrous; ruinous
___ 71. gleamed   C. Dreary; grim
___ 72. sacrifice   D. Hardship; need
___ 73. integrity   E. Biased; intolerant
___ 74. deprivation   F. Offering
___ 75. detection   G. Entered; invaded
___ 76. permeated   H. Discovery
___ 77. prejudiced   I. Honor; decency

VOCABULARY ANSWER KEY - *Number the Stars*

Chapters 1,2
1. C
2. K
3. G
4. L
5. A
6. I
7. F
8. B
9. D
10. J
11. H
12. E

Chapters 3,4
13. C
14. F
15. E
16. L
17. B
18. G
19. K
20. J
21. I
22. A
23. D
24. H

Chapters 5,6
25. H
26. E
27. G
28. C
29. J
30. D
31. B
32. F
33. I
34. A

Chapters 7, 8
35. H
36. I
37. G
38. E
39. D
40. J
41. C
42. A
43. B
44. F

Chapters 9,10,11
45. F
46. I
47. H
48. G
49. J
50. L
51. D
52. C
53. B
54. E
55. A
56. K

Chapters 12,13,14,15
57. G
58. D
59. H
60. A
61. E
62. B
63. C
64. F
65. K
66. L
67. J
68. I

Chapters 16,17 & Afterword
69. B
70. C
71. A
72. F
73. I
74. D
75. H
76. G
77. E

DAILY LESSONS

LESSON ONE

Objectives
1. To give students background information for *Number the Stars*
2. To give students the opportunity to fulfill their nonfiction reading assignment that goes along with this unit
3. To give students practice using library resources
4. To prepare students for the introductory activity in Lesson Two.
5. To give students the opportunity to write to inform by developing and organizing facts to convey information.

Activity

Assign one of each of the following topics to each of your students. Distribute Writing Assignment #1. Discuss the directions in detail. Take your students to the library so they may work on the assignment. Students should fill out a "Nonfiction Assignment Sheet" for at least one of the sources they used, and students should submit these sheets with their compositions.

Topics
1. List the basic beliefs of the Jewish religion.
2. Define anti-Semitism.
3. What was the Holocaust?
4. What is meant by Nazi occupation?
5. Write a short biography on King Christian X of Denmark.
6. Explain what the Danish Resistance was.
7. Write a short biography of Adolf Hitler.
8. Explain what a Nazi was.
9. Make a timeline of World War II.
10. Who were the Allies and name their leaders.
11. Name the Axis countries and their leaders.
12. What was a concentration camp?
13. Where were concentration camps located?
14. What was a Jewish ghetto?
15. When is the Jewish New Year? What does it signify?
16. What was rationing and why was it done? Identify items that were rationed.
17. Identify European countries' boundaries in 1943. Compare to present boundaries.
18. Discover what countries remained neutral during World War II and why.
19. Explain the significance of the Star of David symbol.
20. What is a synagogue and a rabbi?
21. What was Hitler's Final Solution?
22. Locate Denmark on a map and list its surrounding European neighbors and bodies of water.
23. What are blackout curtains and for what were they used?
24. Define sabotage and give examples of its use in World War II.
25. What is a swatiska and what does it mean?

WRITING ASSIGNMENT #1 - *Number the Stars*

PROMPT

You are going to read about Annemarie Johansen and her Jewish friend, Ellen Rosen and their families. They live in Nazi-occupied Denmark during World War II. It is realistic or historical fiction (the events in the novel *could* have taken place, but the characters and events are *fictional*). Before you read it, however, you should have some background information about some of the things mentioned in the story.

You have been assigned one topic about which you must find information. You are to read as much as you can about that topic and write a composition in which you relate what you have learned from your reading. Note that this is a *composition*, not just a sentence or two.

PREWRITING

You will go to the library. When you get there, use the library's resources to find information about your topic. Look for books, encyclopedias, articles in magazines- anything that will give you the information you require. Take a few notes as you read to help you remember important dates, names, places, or other details that will be important in your composition.

After you have gathered information and become well-read on the subject of your report, make a little outline, putting your facts in order.

DRAFTING

You will need an introductory paragraph in which you introduce your topic.

In the body of your composition, put the "meat" of your research- the facts you found- in paragraph form. Each paragraph should have a topic sentence (a sentence letting the reader know what the paragraph will be about) followed by an explanation, examples or details.

Write a concluding paragraph in which you summarize the information you found and conclude your report.

PROMPT

After you have finished a rough draft of your paper, revise it yourself until you are happy with your work. Then, ask a student who sits near you to tell you what he/she likes best about your work, and what things he/she thinks can be improved. Take another look at your composition, keeping in mind your critic's suggestions, and make the revisions you feel are necessary.

PROOFREADING

Do a final proofreading of your paper double-checking your grammar, spelling, organization, and the clarity of your ideas.

NONFICTION ASSIGNMENT SHEET
(To be completed after reading the required nonfiction article)

Name _____ Date _____

Title of Nonfiction Read _____

Written By _____ Publication Date _____

I. Factual Summary: Write a short summary of the piece you read.

II. Vocabulary
    1. With which vocabulary words in the piece did you encounter some degree of difficulty?

    2. How did you resolve your lack of understanding with these words?

III. Interpretation: What was the main point the author wanted you to get from reading his work?

IV. Criticism
    1. With which points of the piece did you agree or find easy to accept? Why?

    2. With which points of the piece did you disagree or find difficult to believe? Why?

V. Personal Response: What do you think about this piece? <u>OR</u> How does this piece influence your ideas?

LESSON TWO

Objectives
1. To introduce The *Number the Stars* unit
2. To distribute books and other related materials
3. To check students' nonfiction reading assignments
4. To model effective oral reading skills by reading aloud pages 1-5
5. To have students identify setting and point of view

Note: Prior to this class period, you need to have put up a bulletin board titled: Little Denmark ; Big War (or something else appropriate). Include a map of Denmark, showing its relationship to Norway, Sweden, Germany, etc. If you do not have a bulletin board to use, use a big sheet of paper put over the chalkboard or a flip-chart style paper on an easel.

Activity #1
Provide students with a plain file card, posterboard strip, or something similar. Have each of them write one fact he/she learned from his/her research. Students could briefly illustrate their fact card, if time allows. Have students one by one, bring their fact up to the bulletin board and post it. Encourage placement for an attractive display. Students could also write directly on the bulletin board paper. After they have placed their fact up, have them share what they learned from their research. Discuss each fact briefly as it is presented so all students will be exposed to a wide variety of background information before reading.

TRANSITION: After all students have had the opportunity to share, ask students what they think it would have been like to live in a Nazi-occupied country in Europe during World War II, especially if they were Jewish? Next ask them, how would they have felt if their best friend was Jewish and they knew the Nazis were relocating them? What would they have done knowing that the Germans punished those who helped Jews? Tell them they will soon see how one such young friend demonstrates her allegiance.

Activity #2
Distribute the materials students will use in this unit. Explain in detail how students are to use these materials.

Study Guides Students should preview the study guide questions before each reading assignment to get a feeling for what events and ideas are important in that section. After reading the section, students will (as a class or individually) answer the questions to review the important events and ideas from that section of the book. Students should keep the study guides as study materials for the unit test.

<u>Vocabulary</u> Prior to reading a reading assignment, students will do vocabulary work related to the section of the book they are about to read. Following the completion of the reading of the book, there will be a vocabulary review of all the words used in the vocabulary assignments. Students should keep their vocabulary work as study materials for the unit test.

<u>Reading Assignment Sheet</u> You need to fill in the reading assignment sheet to let students know when their reading has to be completed. You can either write the assignment sheet on a side blackboard or bulletin board and leave it there for students to see each day, or you can "ditto" copies for each student to have. In either case, you should advise students to become very familiar with the reading assignments so they know what is expected of them.

<u>Extra Activities Center</u> The Extra Activities page in this unit contains suggestions for a library of related books and articles in your classroom as well as crossword and word search puzzles. Make an extra activities center in your room where you will keep these materials for students to use. (Bring the books and articles in from the library and keep several copies of the puzzles on hand.) Explain to students that these materials are available for students to use when they finish reading assignments or other class work early.

<u>Books</u> Each school has its own rules and regulations regarding student use of school books. Advise students of the procedures that are normal for your school.

<u>Activity #3</u>

Have students examine cover of book and turn to the opening chapter. Read these five pages to them as they follow along. Identify the use of third person narration, and discuss specifics of the Copenhagen setting. Assign P,V,R for Chapters 1 and 2.

LESSON THREE

Objectives
1. To review the main events and vocabulary from chapters 1 and 2
2. To preview the study questions for chapters 3 and 4
3. To familiarize students with the vocabulary in chapters 3 and 4
4. To begin the reading of chapter 3

Activity #1

Discuss the answers to the study questions for chapters 1 and 2 in detail. Write the answers on the board or overhead transparency so students can have the correct answers for study purposes. Note: It is a good practice in public speaking and leadership skills for individual students to take charge of leading the discussions of the study questions. Perhaps a different student could go to the front of the class and lead the discussion each day that the study questions are discussed during this unit. Of course, the teacher should guide the discussion when appropriate and be sure to fill in any gaps the students leave.

Activity #2

Give students the remaining class time to preview the study questions for chapters 3 and 4 of *Number the Stars* and to do the related vocabulary work. If time allows, begin reading chapter 3 or assign the reading of chapters 3 and 4 to be completed prior to the next class session.

LESSON FOUR

Objectives
1. To review the main events and ideas from chapters 3 and 4
2. To practice identifying characters by what they have said
3. To familiarize students with vocabulary from chapters 5 and 6
4. To preview study questions for chapters 5 and 6

Activity #1
Discuss the answers to the study questions for chapters 3 and 4 as you have done the study questions previously.

Activity #2
Allow each student to select a partner. Have them take turns reading quotes to each other to identify the speaker out of chapters 3 and 4. They could refer to the other two chapters, as well. Encourage them to try to sound like the person whose quote it is by acting some out yourself and having them guess.

Activity #3
Have students look over the prereading vocabulary work for chapters 5 and 6 for about 10 minutes. Use the matching section of the vocabulary pages as a springboard for a game similar to Concentration. Divide students into groups of four or five. Have students quickly copy the vocabulary words (divide the task into sections to expedite) and their clues on separate index cards. Turn them all over, after mixing them up. Have students in small groups take turns flipping over two of the cards. If they are a match, i.e. a vocabulary word matches with its meaning, they keep the pair and get another turn. Students may look at the vocabulary words in their sentences for contextual clues. Continue play until all cards are matched into sets. Play again, if time.

Activity #4
Give students any remaining time to look over study questions for chapters 5 and 6. Assign reading of these two chapters to be done prior to the next class session.

NOTE: Explain to students that you will be having writing conferences in the next class session. During the writing conference, you will discuss their writing skills individually, based on their first writing assignment in this unit (World War II information).

LESSON FIVE

Objectives
1. To review the main events and ideas of chapters 5 and 6
2. To evaluate students' writing
3. To have students revise their Writing Assignment 1 papers

Activity #1
    Use the multiple choice format of the study guide questions for chapters 5 and 6 as a quiz to check that students have done the required reading and to review the main ideas of chapters 5 and 6. Exchange papers for checking. Discuss answers and make sure students take notes for studying purposes.

Activity #2
    Assign the prereading vocabulary pages, study guide questions and reading of chapters 7 and 8. Students should work on this while they are waiting for their conference with you.

Activity #3
    Call students to your desk (or some other private area) to discuss their papers from Writing Assignment 1. Use the following Writing Evaluation Form to help structure your conference. Give students a date when their revisions are due.

WRITING EVALUATION FORM - *Number the Stars*

Name _____ Date _____

Writing Assignment #1 for the *Number the Stars* unit   Grade _____

Circle One For Each Item:

Description (paragraph 1)	excellent	good	fair	poor
Plans (body paragraphs)	excellent	workable	fair	not realistic
Conclusion	excellent	good	fair	poor
Grammar:	excellent	good	fair	poor
Spelling:	excellent	good	fair	poor
Punctuation:	excellent	good	fair	poor
Legibility:	excellent	good	fair	poor

Strengths:

Weaknesses:

Comments/Suggestions:

LESSON SIX

Objectives
1. To review the main ideas of chapters 7 and 8
2. To give students the opportunity to practice writing to express personal ideas

Activity #1

Hand out four little slips of paper or mini cards to each student that have the letters A,B,C, or D on them. A good idea is to use different color cards for each letter. Use the multiple choice study guide questions and answers on Chapters 7 and 8 for an oral review. Read the question (and/ or show it on the overhead). Then give students the four possible answers, labeling them A, B, C, or D (or show on overhead again). Students respond by holding up the card with what they think is the correct answer. This is one variety of Every Student Response. Remind students not to look at what others are holding up, but to simply display the card of their choice. This is a quick indicator of students' comprehension. You can make it somewhat different by requiring complete silence and having them read the questions silently from the overhead, or make it more mysterious (fun?) by blindfolding everyone and have them hold up a certain number of fingers per answer instead of using the cards.

Activity #2

Distribute Writing Assignment #2 and discuss the directions in detail. Allow the remaining class time for students to complete the assignment. Give them specifics of when final copies are due to you.

WRITING ASSIGNMENT #2 - *Number the Stars*

PROMPT

Now that you have finished reading chapters seven and eight, you know that Ellen has seen the sea for the first time. Her family stays mostly in the city, so she is amazed by the size of the sea that she and Annemarie view. She calls it a 'whole world of water'.

Your assignment is to recreate on paper, that very special first time you too, saw the sea. If you have never been to the ocean, write about the first time you saw some other natural geographical phenomenon. Your goal is to capture the feelings and sensations you had when you first *saw* the ocean, the *smell*, the *sound* of the water or seagulls, the *feel* of the sand or waves, and even the *taste* of the salt air. Essentially, recreate this event using all your senses.

PREWRITING

The first thing you need to do is close your eyes and try to recall everything you can remember about this event. After you have recreated this in your mind, jot down and list everything that came to you as you were recreating this event in your mind. Then, you may want to make a web (shaped like a sun) for each sense (i.e. sound, etc.) Place the sense in the center circle, and list everything you can associate with that sense on the lines radiating from the center. In this way, you will have some organization to your prewriting.

DRAFTING

Begin your paper with an introductory paragraph giving your audience some background on where, when, and with whom you visited an ocean. Tell what ocean you went to, include if it was part of a vacation, a field trip, or whatever is appropriate. This paragraph's purpose is to lead into the body of your composition, which is coming next.

The body of your composition should contain the information you generated from your prewriting. Begin with one of the sets of feelings, thoughts, and ideas you came up with for one of the senses. Continue until you have covered each of them adequately.

Finish your composition with a concluding paragraph in which you express any final observations or memories or make some personal comment about this event, such as Ellen did when she summed up her vision.

PROMPT

When you finish your rough draft, ask a student who sits near you to read it. After reading your rough draft, he/she should tell you what he/she liked best about your work, which parts were difficult to understand, and ways in which your work could be improved. Reread your paper considering your critic's comments and make the corrections you think are necessary.

PROOFREADING

Do a final proofreading of your paper double-checking your grammar, spelling, organization, and the clarity of your ideas.

LESSON SEVEN

Objectives
1. To preview the study questions for chapters 9-11
2. To familiarize students with the vocabulary for chapters 9-11
3. To read chapters 9-11
4. To give students practice reading orally
5. To evaluate students' oral reading

Activity #1

Have students pair up. Within their pairs, have them look over the study questions for chapters 9, 10, and 11. Also have them do the prereading vocabulary work together.
Ask students to begin partner reading (reading back and forth with their partner quietly) until all students have completed the required work. When all students have finished objectives 1 and 2, move on to Activity #2.

Activity #2

Have students read chapters 9, 10, and 11 orally in class. You probably know the best way to get readers within your class; pick students at random, ask for volunteers, have students who have just read select another student, assign numbers to students and spin a spinner, or whatever works best for you. Complete the oral reading evaluation form that follows this lesson after listening to your students read.

ORAL READING EVALUATION - *Number the Stars*

Name _____ Class____ Date _____

SKILL	EXCELLENT	GOOD	AVERAGE	FAIR	POOR
Fluency	5	4	3	2	1
Clarity	5	4	3	2	1
Audibility	5	4	3	2	1
Pronunciation	5	4	3	2	1
_____	5	4	3	2	1
_____	5	4	3	2	1

Total _____ Grade _____

Comments:

LESSON EIGHT

Objectives
1. To introduce simile, personification, and metaphor as figures of speech
2. To distinguish between three different types of figurative language
3. To have students locate figurative language in the text
4. To create original figures of speech
5. To illustrate figurative language

Activity #1
      Tell the class you are going to read a few phrases to them from their most recently read chapters in the book. Ask them to listen carefully and try to identify similarities between them or see if they can identify what they are examples of:
>-Blossom moved her mouth like an old woman adjusting her false teeth.
>-His strong hands continued, deftly pressing like a pulse against the cow.
>-She entered, held tightly like a little girl, her bare legs dangling, against her father's chest.
>-It was as if Ellen had moved now into a different world.
>-She heard- as if in a recurring nightmare- the pounding on the door.

These examples all happen to be similes. Point out the use of *like* and *as* to create the comparisons. When ready, move on to Activity #2

Activity #2
      Make three columns on the chalkboard labeling each one separately: simile, metaphor, and personification. Spend some time here instructing about the other two forms of figurative language. You could use specific examples from the following test, focusing on the ones from earlier chapters (# 22 and above). Perhaps you could cite some examples from familiar songs. Ask why they think any author or lyricist would use them? Do they use them? Why? In what way does using them enhance speaking or writing or the understanding of each of these. As a whole group, have students give you examples they can think of and then have them locate a few in any part of the text they have read. Allow them to come to the board and write these under the correct heading. When you are satisfied with their ability to recognize them and differentiate between them, go to the next activity.

Activity #3
Divide the class into small groups of three or four. Have each group assign a recorder. Give them a couple of sheets of paper. Ask each group to locate as many of these figures of speech as they can from the text. They may be more successful in the portion they already have read, but it isn't necessary to limit them. Giving them a time constraint is an option. It could be a race, you are the judge. You may want to rule out using the ones that are posted on the board. It's up to you. Wrap this activity up by having the group with the **most** read their list aloud. Decide as a whole group if indeed each one is correct. Have all groups check off the ones that are read that they also found. Allow every group to read any that have not yet been mentioned. You could give small treats for first, second, third place, etc.

Activity #4
Have students create one example of each type. They could be individual sentences or you could require them to write a short paragraph using all three. Base this on the ability level of your students and/or time. Create one together as a model. If time, have them illustrate it with original art work or magazine pictures. Save finished products for display. They could do this part as homework.

NOTE: The following figurative language test is optional. You may want to use it right after instruction, later in this unit, or not at all. You may choose to use it only as a resource for this lesson. It contains examples from the entire book.

FIGURATIVE LANGUAGE TEST - *Number the Stars*

I. Read the following examples of figurative language. Label each one separately with either an **S** for simile, **P** for personification, or an **M** for metaphor. **BONUS**: Circle the four that are more than one type.

1. He said I looked like his little girl. _____
2. Halte! The German word was as familiar as it was frightening._____
3. For Kirsti, the soldiers were simply a part of the landscape, something that had always been there as unimportant as lampposts. _____
4. You look like hoodlums when you run._____
5. She is pretty, like my own little girl. _____
6. She imagined the pink strip of Norway crushed by a fist . _____
7. It sounded like a very brave answer._____
8. All of Denmark is his bodyguard._____
9. They said he was like a son._____
10. Well now, I think that all of Denmark should be bodyguard for the Jews, as well._____
11. I remember it was raining. Mama was crying, and the rain made it seem as if the whole world was crying._____
12. But still, it wouldn't be as bad as being dead. _____
13. Dangers were no more than odd imaginings, like ghost stories that children made up to frighten one another: things that couldn't possibly happen. _____
14. High against the pale clouds, seagulls soared and cried out as if they were in mourning.____
15. The meadow ended at the sea, and the gray water licked there at damp brown grass flattened by the wind and bordered by smooth, heavy stones.._____
16. I mean the real sea, the way it is here. Open like this- a whole world of water._____
17. For a moment, to Annemarie, listening, it seemed like all the earlier times._____
18. He looks as if he would run and hide if there were a thunderstorm._____
19. I suppose that if they knew Henrik had kept this tiny bit, they would come with guns and march it away, down the path._____
20. The three of them pictured a mound of frightened butter under military arrest._____
21. Now, the specter of guns and grim-faced soldiers seemed nothing more than a ghost story.__
22. To lie at anchor, hearing the sea slap against the sides._____
23. Blossom looked up at Annemarie with big brown eyes, and moved her wrinkled mouth like an old woman adjusting false teeth.._____
24. His strong hands continued, deftly pressing like a pulse against the cow.._____
25. The pinkish light of sunset fell in irregular shapes upon the stacked hay._____
26. The old man bent his head forward and closed his eyes, as if he were praying. _____
27. But in a moment the door opened and she returned- held tightly like a little girl._____
28. She fell asleep, and it was a sleep as thin as the night clouds, dotted with dreams that came and went like the stars._____
29. Your proper Mama, crawling inch by inch! I probably looked like a drunkard._____
30. I know the way, and it's almost light now. I can run like the wind._____

Figurative Language Test Page 2

II. List one example of your own for each type of figurative language. They can be original or from your favorite songs or poetry.

III. Illustrate your favorite example of figurative language from those listed.

ANSWER KEY: FIGURATIVE LANGUAGE TEST - *Number the Stars*

I.
1. S
2. S
3. S
4. S
5. S
6. P
7. S
8. M
9. S
10. M
11. S, P
12. S
13. M, S
14. P, S
15. P
16. M
17. S
18. S
19. P
20. P
21. M
22. P
23. S
24. S
25. P
26. S
27. S
28. S, P
29. S
30. S

II. Answers will vary.

III. Creative response.

LESSON NINE

Objectives
    1. To review main events and ideas in chapters 9, 10, and 11
    2. To do the prereading vocabulary work for chapters 12-15
    3. To preview study guide questions for chapters 12-15

Activity #1
    Use the multiple choice study guide questions as a quiz to test students' reading of assigned text and as a review of the main ideas. Exchange papers to check. Discuss answers to insure understanding. Encourage note taking for their later study use.

Activity #2
    Have students spend about 10 minutes completing the prereading vocabulary page. After they have done that, pair them up. Have one member of each pair "act" out one of the words, while the other one tries to guess the word. Do this until all of the vocabulary words have been covered at least once. Students could be in small groups, as well. This is similar to the game Charades.

Activity #3
    Have students preview study guide questions and begin reading independently chapters 12-15 in the remaining class time.

LESSON TEN

Objectives
    1. To review the main ideas and events in chapters 12, 13, 14, and 15
    2. To give students practice in writing to persuade

Activity #1
    Divide the class into two teams. Play a game like a spelling bee, but instead of spelling a word, they must answer one of the questions correctly. Using the study guide questions for chapters 12-15, begin play. 1. Determine which team goes first. 2. Read one of the questions for one team member to answer. 3. If it was answered correctly, that team gets a point. 4. If it was not answered correctly, the other team gets a try at the same question. 5. Question goes back and forth until it is answered correctly. 6. Read another question, and repeat earlier play. 7. Continue until all questions for chapters 12-15 have been answered correctly. 8. Reward winning team with some small prize or other incentive.

Activity #2
    Distribute Writing Assignment #3 and discuss directions in detail. In the remaining class time, have students begin work on this assignment. Be sure to give students specifics on when assignment is due.

WRITING ASSIGNMENT #3 - *Number the Stars*

PROMPT

Since you have finished reading chapter 15, you know that Annemarie was stopped by a set of Nazi soldiers on the path on her way to the harbor. She had a very important mission to complete in a very short time. It was necessary for her to rush the unopened packet to her uncle because Mr. Rosen had unknowingly dropped it when he tripped on the loose step outside Henrik's house.

In this writing assignment, you are to pretend you are Annemarie on your way to the harbor with the packet concealed in the basket. It is hiding beneath a lunch of bread, an apple and some cheese for your uncle. You are stopped by the Nazi soldiers, and it is your job to convince them to allow you to continue your journey to your fisherman uncle whose has forgotten his lunch. You know you need to get there quickly, before the boat leaves.

PREWRITING

To begin with, list any and all possible arguments you can think that you could use in this instance. Decide which are your strongest justifiable arguments, and which are less substantial. Organize your points from weaker to strongest and jot down anything you can think of which will support or explain your arguments.

DRAFTING

Begin with an introductory paragraph in which you express your frustration and discontent on being stopped on your way to deliver your uncle's forgotten lunch. Follow that with one paragraph for each of the main points you have to support your argument to convince them to let you go as swiftly as possible, without drawing attention to the packet. Fill in each paragraph with reasons and feelings that support your main point. Then, write an ending paragraph that summarizes your frustration and need to be on your way as your final statement.

PROMPT

When you finish the rough draft of your paper, ask a student who sits near you to read it. After reading your rough draft, he/she should tell you what he/she liked best about your work, which parts were difficult to understand, and ways in which your work could be improved. Reread your paper considering your critic's comments, and make the corrections you think are necessary.

PROOFREADING

Do a final proofreading of your paper double-checking your grammar, spelling, organization, and the clarity of your ideas.

LESSON ELEVEN

Objectives
1. To preview the study guide questions for chapters 16 and 17
2. To practice making predictions
3. To do the prereading vocabulary work for chapters 16 and 17
4. To read orally chapters 16 and 17
5. To discuss the theme of bravery

Activity #1

Have students pair up and look over study guide questions 1-9. After they look over them, tell them to write down what they predict will be the answers to the questions. Have each partner predict half of the answers. Ask them to jot down their answers on a single piece of paper and put away temporarily.

Activity #2

Have students spend less than 5 minutes completing the prereading vocabulary work independently for words # 1-3 only. Pass out plain paper for drawing, or use individual easels or slates. Have students select a new partner for this activity. Have one of the partners sketch their impression of one of the vocabulary words within a limited amount of time. The other one is to guess which vocabulary word he/she is trying to picture. When the correct word has been chosen, play turns to the other partner. Continue play until the 3 vocabulary words have been covered. This is similar to the game Pictionary. It could also be done in small groups.

Activity #3

Have students read chapters 16 and 17 orally in class. Refer to Lesson Seven for ideas in motivation. Once they complete the reading, have them retrieve their predictions made in Activity #1 and compare their answers with what they just discovered in their reading. Ask how many they were able to get correct. Discuss how bravery is depicted in chapter 16. Allow students to share their acts of bravery, or their impression of others' bravery.

Activity #4

Assign previewing of Study Guide Questions (questions 10-12) and Prereading vocabulary work (#4-9) on the Afterword to be completed by next class. Inform class that they will be using the vocabulary in an activity in the next lesson.

LESSON TWELVE

Objectives
1. To practice vocabulary from the Afterword
2. To read the Afterword orally
3. To reinforce the true aspects of this novel
4. To review the main events and ideas from chapters 16 and 17 & Afterword

Activity #1
Have students glance over the vocabulary from the Afterword #4-9. (They were to have reviewed for homework.) Write each of the six words on the chalkboard, leaving space beneath each one. Divide the class into six teams. Have each team list as many synonyms for their word as they can come up with, beneath it, on the chalkboard. Give them a time limit and reward the team who comes up with the most correct synonyms. It is up to you if you want them to be able to refer to a thesaurus or dictionary first.

Activity #2
Read the Afterword together orally. Thoughtfully discuss the author's presentation of research and how she was able to weave these elements into this story. Encourage reading other stories of Resistance during World War II, if they are interested. Many of the facts used in *Number the Stars* can be found in a nonfiction book by Harold Flender called *Rescue in Denmark*. Another nonfiction resource would be Milton Meltzer's *Rescue- the Story of How Gentiles Saved Jews During the Holocaust*.

Activity #3
Give students the multiple choice study guide questions as a quiz to test their comprehension of the last two lessons' material and to review the main events and ideas from chapters 16, 17 and Afterword. Have students exchange papers to check. Encourage note-taking for later use.

LESSONS THIRTEEN AND FOURTEEN

Objectives
1. To discuss the ideas and themes from Number the Stars in greater detail
2. To have students exercise their interpretive and critical thinking skills
3. To try to relate some of the ideas in *Number the Stars* to the students' lives

Activity #1

Choose the questions from the Extra Discussion Questions/Writing Assignments which seem most appropriate for your students. A class discussion of these questions is most effective if students have been given the opportunity to formulate answers to the questions prior to the discussion. To this end, you may either have all the students formulate answers to all the questions, divide your class into groups and assign one or more questions to each group, or you could assign one question to each student in your class. The option you choose will make a difference in the amount of class time needed for this activity.

Activity #2

After students have had ample time to formulate answers to the questions, begin your class discussion of the questions and the ideas presented by the questions. Be sure students take notes during the discussion so they have information to study for the unit test.

EXTRA DISCUSSION QUESTIONS/WRITING ASSIGNMENTS
Number the Stars

Interpretive
1. From what point of view is the story written? How does that affect our attitudes as we read?

2. Identify the setting and tell how it dictates this story.

3. What are the main conflicts in the story and how are they resolved?

4. What is foreshadowing? Give examples of foreshadowing used in *Number the Stars*.

5. Based on the facts in the story, can you determine the year and month most of this story takes place? Over what amount of time does the entire story span from beginning to end?

6. Give a complete character analysis of Annemarie.

7. Explain the meaning of each chapter title.

8. Analyze the qualities and character traits of these characters: Kirsti, Ellen, Mrs. Johansen, Uncle Henrik, and Peter. How do the roles they play differ?

9. How are the Nazi soldiers portrayed by the author? Do any of them share any qualities of any of the other characters?

10. Define climax. Next, summarize the main events leading up to **it** and the remaining events after **it** that create the resolution.

11. Annemarie finds out at the end of the story that Peter was in the Resistance. What earlier clues (foreshadowing) were there that Peter was a part of the Resistance?

Critical
12. Explain the significance of the title "*Number the Stars* ".

13. Why does Mama offer to open the casket when she knows exactly what is inside?

14. Compare and contrast life in Europe during World War II with life there now.

15. Why was it necessary for Mama, Papa, and Uncle Henrik to talk in codes?

Number the Stars Extra Discussion Questions page 2

16. How might the story have changed if Annemarie had not removed Ellen's necklace?

17. What significance is there in the gift of seashells that Peter brought for Annemarie and Kirsti?

18. Contrast Peter's behavior and personality *before* and *after* Lise's death.

19. Why did the young boy say that "all of Denmark" was King Christian's bodyguard?

20. Why do you think the author introduced the death of Annemarie's older sister into the plot?

21. Describe Lois Lowry's writing style, including her use of figurative language. How does it shape the reader's perception of the story?

22. Is the story of *Number the Stars* believable? Why or why not?

23. Compose another title for this novel. What part of the novel lead you to come up with it?

24. What universal themes are present in *Number the Stars*?

25. Compare and contrast celebrations held for a calendar New Year and the Jewish New Year.

26. Can you identify any situation/s in the world today where one group of people is the victim of oppression or discrimination by their government? Is there evidence of any resistance groups fighting for these victimized people? If so, compare their tactics to those used by the Danish.

Critical/ Personal Response

27. Do you think the pretend funeral was a good idea? Explain your opinion. Can you think of another idea or make any improvements or additions to the idea to make it safer?

28. Have you read any other books written by Lois Lowry? How do they compare to *Number the Stars*? Which one is your favorite? Why?

29. Why do you think the soldier slapped Mama? If you would have been Annemarie, how would you have reacted when the Nazi soldier slapped your mother?

30. What makes Annemarie and her parents 'good friends' of the Rosens? Who are you 'good friends' with? Would you do what the Johansens did to help them? Why or why not?

Number the Stars Extra Discussion Questions page 3

31. While taking the basket to Uncle Henrik, Annemarie tells herself the story of "Little Red Riding Hood". Why do you think she did that? Have you ever been scared and done something similar? Please share.

Personal Response

32. Describe how you would have felt if you were Ellen and had to stay with a friend, pretending to be her dead sister. In addition to being displaced, you don't know where your parents are.

33. Uncle Henrik gives his impression of what bravery is. Explain your definition of bravery, giving examples to support it.

34. How would you have taken care of your Jewish friend's things and place while they were gone? Explain how you would have welcomed them back after the war ended.

35. Annemarie gets frustrated with her little sister at times. If you have a younger sibling, how do you keep from getting impatient with him/her? When you do become frustrated how do you cope?

36. The Danish people had a central place in Copenhagen where they could go for fun. Where do you go that is similar to Tivoli Gardens? What do you like to do there? Are there fireworks?

37. Mama and the girls take a train ride from Copenhagen to the shore. Have you ever taken a train ride? What was it like? Compare it to two other forms of transportation.

38. Have you read any other historical fiction from this time period? If so, name them. In what ways were they similar to or different from *Number the Stars*?

39. Ellen's father wants her to be a teacher, like him. She hopes to convince him otherwise. Have you ever experienced a parental expectation that is different from your desire? Explain. How did you deal with it?

40. The entire Jewish population was discriminated against in Europe during this time period. Share a time you felt you were discriminated against. Why did you feel you were treated differently and how did you respond?

41. Compare and contrast the Jewish religion with your family's religion.

42. If you had been living in Europe during this time period, would you have been a member of a resistance group? Why or why not? What qualities would you have had to possess?

Number the Stars Extra Discussion Questions Page 4

Quotations

1. "Go home, all of you. Go study your school books. And don't run. You look like hoodlums when you run."

2. "He'll remember *my* face, Mama, because he said I look like *his* little girl. He said I was pretty."

3. " All of Denmark is his bodyguard."

4. "Yes, It is true. Any Danish citizen would die for King Christian, to protect him."

5. "The whole world has changed, only the fairy tales remain the same."

6. "It is their way of tormenting. For some reason, they want to torment Jewish people. It has happened in other countries. They have taken their time here- have let us relax a little. But now it seems to be starting."

7. "Well, now I think that all of Denmark must be bodyguard for the Jews, as well."

8. "It was my birthday. I woke up in the night and I could hear the booms. And there were lights in the sky. Mama said it was fireworks for my birthday!"

9. "No. It' s the Jewish New Year. That's just for us . But if you want, Kirsti, you can come that night and watch Mama light the candles."

10. "Go, now, and get your nightgowns. It will be a long night."

11. "Don't be frightened, once I had three daughters. Tonight I am proud to have three daughters again."

12. "My father wants me to be teacher. He wants *everyone* to be a teacher, like him. But maybe I can convince him that I should go to acting school. "

13. "I remember it was raining, it was still raining the next morning when Mama told me. Mama was crying, and the rain made it seem as if the whole *world* was crying."

14. "She would have looked so beautiful in her wedding dress. She had such a pretty smile. I used to pretend that she was *my* sister, too. "

15. "I can't get it open! I never take it off- I can't even remember how to open it!"

Number the Stars Extra Discussion Questions Page 5

16. "Where did you get the dark-haired one? From a different father? From the milkman?"

17. "You will see each of my daughters, each with her name written on the photograph."

18. "If only I go with the girls, it will be safer. They are unlikely to suspect a woman and her children. But if they are watching us- if they see all of us leave? If they are aware that the apartment is empty, that you don't go to your office this morning? Then they will know."

19. "So, Henrik, is the weather good for fishing?"

20. "Are you visiting your brother for the New Year?"

21. "I had named him Trofast- faithful. And it was just the right name for him, because what a faithful dog he was ! Every afternoon he was right here, waiting for me to return. He knew that right time, somehow. Sometimes, as I come around this bend, even today, I feel as if I might come upon Trofast, waiting still, with his tail wagging."

22. "Run ahead and tell the house we've brought a friend."

23. "I mean the real sea, the way it is here. Open like this- a whole world of water."

24. "I wish I knew where my parents are."

25. "And I have named him Thor, for the God of Thunder."

26. "They relocate all the farmer's butter, right into the stomach of their army! I suppose that if they knew Henrik had kept this tiny bit, they would come with guns and march it away, down the path."

27. "The God of Thunder has made a very small rain shower in the corner of the kitchen floor. Keep an eye on him."

28. "Tomorrow will be a day for fishing."

29. "But, it is much *easier* to be brave if you do not know everything. And so your Mama does not know everything. Neither do I. We know only what we need to know.

30. "And I know it is the custom to pay one's respects by looking your loved one in the face. It seems odd to me that you have closed this coffin up so tightly."

Number the Stars Extra Discussion Questions Page 6

31. "The doctor said it should be closed, because Aunt Birte died of typhus, and he said that there was a chance the germs would still be there, would still be dangerous. But what does he know- only a country doctor, an old man at that? Surely typhus germs wouldn't linger in a dead person! An d dear Aunt Birte; I have been longing to see her face, to kiss her goodbye. Of course we will open he casket! "

32. "I know the way, and it's almost light now. I can run like the wind.

33. "Don't! That's Uncle Henrik's bread! My mother baked it!"

34. "Go on to your uncle and tell him the German dogs enjoyed his bread."

35. "There are many soldiers in Gilleleje and all along the coast. They are searching all the boats now. They know that the Jews are escaping, but they are not sure how, and they rarely find them. The hiding places are carefully concealed, and we often pile dead fish on the deck as well. They hate getting their shiny boots dirty!"

36. "And they have created a special drug. I don't know what it is, but it was in the handkerchief. It attracts the dogs, but when they sniff at it, it ruins their sense of smell. Imagine that!"

37. "You will, little one. You saved her life, after all. Someday you will find her again. Someday the war will end, all wars do."

38. "Until then, I will wear it myself."

LESSON FIFTEEN

<u>Objectives</u>
To review all of the vocabulary work done in this unit

<u>Activity</u>
Choose one (or more) of the vocabulary review activities listed on the next page(s) and spend your class period as directed in the activity. Some of the materials for these review activities are located in the Vocabulary Resource section of this unit.

VOCABULARY REVIEW ACTIVITIES

1. Divide your class into two teams and have an old-fashioned spelling or definition bee.

2. Give each of your students (or students in groups of two, three or four) a *Number the Stars* Vocabulary Word Search Puzzle. The person (group) to find all of the vocabulary words in the puzzle first wins.

3. Give students a *Number the Stars* Vocabulary Word Search Puzzle without the word list. The person or group to find the most vocabulary words in the puzzle wins.

4. Use a *Number the Stars* Vocabulary Crossword Puzzle. Put the puzzle onto a transparency on the overhead projector (so everyone can see it), and do the puzzle together as a class.

5. Give students a *Number the Stars* Vocabulary Matching Worksheet to do.

6. Divide your class into two teams. Use the *Number the Stars* vocabulary words with their letters jumbled as a word list. Student 1 from Team A faces off against Student 1 from Team B. You write the first jumbled word on the board. The first student (1A or 1B) to unscramble the word wins the chance for his/her team to score points. If 1A wins the jumble, go to student 2A and give him/her a definition. He/she must give you the correct spelling of the vocabulary word which fits that definition. If he/she does, Team A scores a point, and you give student 3A a definition for which you expect a correctly spelled matching vocabulary word. Continue giving Team A definitions until some team member makes an incorrect response. An incorrect response sends the game back to the jumbled-word face off, this time with students 2A and 2B. Instead of repeating giving definitions to the first few students of each team, continue with the student after the one who gave the last incorrect response on the team. For example, if Team B wins the jumbled-word face-off, and student 5B gave the last incorrect answer for Team B, you would start this round of definition questions with student 6B, and so on. The team with the most points wins!

7. Have students write a story in which they correctly use as many vocabulary words as possible. Have students read their compositions orally. Post the most original compositions on your bulletin board.

LESSON SIXTEEN

Objective
To review the main ideas presented in *Number the Stars*

Activity #1
Choose one of the review games/activities included in this guide and spend your class period as outlined there. Some materials for these activities are located in the Unit Resource section of this unit.

Activity #2
Remind students that the Unit Test will be in the next class meeting. Stress the review of the Study Guides and their class notes as a last minute, brush-up review for the unit test.

REVIEW GAMES/ACTIVITIES - *Number the Stars*

1. Ask the class to make up a unit test for *Number the Stars*. The test should have 4 sections: matching, true/false, short answer, and essay. Students may use 1/2 period to make the test and then swap papers and use the other 1/2 class period to take a test a classmate has devised. (open book) You may want to use the unit test included in this guide or take questions from the students' unit tests to formulate your own test.

2. Take 1/2 period for students to make up true and false questions (including the answers). Collect the papers and divide the class into two teams. Draw a big tic-tac-toe board on the chalk board. Make one team X and one team O. Ask questions to each side, giving each student one turn. If the question is answered correctly, that students' team's letter (X or O) is placed in the box. If the answer is incorrect, no mark is placed in the box. The object is to get three marks in a row like tic-tac-toe. You may want to keep track of the number of games won for each team.

3. Take 1/2 period for students to make up questions (true/false and short answer). Collect the questions. Divide the class into two teams. You'll alternate asking questions to individual members of teams A & B (like in a spelling bee). The question keeps going from A to B until it is correctly answered, then a new question is asked. A correct answer does not allow the team to get another question. Correct answers are +2 points; incorrect answers are -1 point.

4. Have students pair up and quiz each other from their study guides and class notes.

5. Give students a *Number the Stars* crossword puzzle to complete.

6. Divide your class into two teams. Use the *Number the Stars* crossword words with their letters jumbled as a word list. Student 1 from Team A faces off against Student 1 from Team B. You write the first jumbled word on the board. The first student (1A or 1B) to unscramble the word wins the chance for his/her team to score points. If 1A wins the jumble, go to student 2A and give him/her a clue. He/she must give you the correct word which matches that clue. If he/she does, Team A scores a point, and you give student 3A a clue for which you expect another correct response. Continue giving Team A clues until some team member makes an incorrect response. An incorrect response sends the game back to the jumbled-word face off, this time with students 2A and 2B. Instead of repeating giving clues to the first few students of each team, continue with the student after the one who gave the last incorrect response on the team. For example, if Team B wins the jumbled-word face-off, and student 5B gave the last incorrect answer for Team B, you would start this round of clue questions with student 6B, and so on.

UNIT TESTS

SHORT ANSWER UNIT TEST #1 - *Number the Stars*

I. Matching/Identify

___ 1. Resistance

___ 2. Christian X

___ 3. Peter

___ 4. Great Aunt Birte

___ 5. Sweden

___ 6. Copenhagen

___ 7. kroner

___ 8. typhus

___ 9. handkerchief

___ 10. Ingeborg

___ 11. psalm

___ 12. swastika

___ 13. Gilleleje

___ 14. seasick

___ 15. bodyguard

A. Nazi symbol

B. Works secretly against Nazis

C. Danish money

D. Smuggled Jews out of Denmark

E. Red-headed fiance of Lise

F. How Mrs. Rosen felt in the boat

G. Danish king

H. Great Aunt Birte's cause of death

I. Contains words: It is he who numbers the stars one by one

J. Pretend dead aunt

K. Coast of Denmark near Sweden

L. Jews were taken here by boat

M. All of Denmark is King Christian's

N. Capital of Denmark

O. Annemarie delivered to Uncle Henrik

II. Short Answer
1. Explain what is meant by Nazi occupation.

Number the Stars Short Answer Unit Test 1 Page 2

2. What is the Resistance?

3. Name King Christian's bodyguard.

4. Why did King Christian surrender to the Nazis rather than fight?

5. Why was it frightening to Kirsti for Peter to visit them late at night?

6. Kirsti was told there was a firework display for her birthday. What really was it?

7. What is meant by the term 'relocation'?

8. How does Ellen verbally express the sadness she felt when Annemarie's sister Lise died?

9. What does Annemarie yank from Ellen and why?

Number the Stars Short Answer Unit Test 1 Page 3

10. Why does Mrs. Johansen think her husband should stay home from the trip to her brother's?

11. In what way does Mama warn the girls when they return from looking at the sea?

12. Why is Annemarie angry and confused with her mother and uncle?

13. After Uncle Henrik admits to Annemarie they lied, what reason does he give her?

14. What is Annemarie thinking while Peter reads the psalm aloud?

15. Stripped of all their possessions and acts, what quality does Annemarie still recognize in the Jews as they depart for the boat?

16. While examining her mother's ankle, what does Annemarie find?

17. Why is Annemarie puzzled when she reaches her uncle's boat at the harbor?

Number the Stars Short Answer Unit Test 1 Page 4

18. How does Uncle Henrik explain *brave* to Annemarie?

19. How many more years did the war last?

20. What happened to Peter?

Number the Stars Short Answer Test 1 Page 5

III. Essay

    What is the significance of the title *Number the Stars*? Explain in detail, using specific examples from the story.

IV. Vocabulary

    Listen to the vocabulary word and spell it. After you have spelled all the words, go back and write down the definitions.

1.

2.

3.

4.

5.

6.

7.

8.

9.

10.

SHORT ANSWER UNIT TEST 2 *Number the Stars*

I. Matching/Identify

___ 1. kroner   A. Danish king

___ 2. typhus   B. Red-headed fiance of Lise

___ 3. Copenhagen   C. Pretend dead aunt

___ 4. Great Aunt Birte   D. Jews were taken here by boat

___ 5. Gilleleje   E. Works secretly against Nazis

___ 6. swastika   F. How Mrs. Rosen felt in the boat

___ 7. Resistance   G. Coast of Denmark near Sweden

___ 8. Christian X   H. Great Aunt Birte's cause of death

___ 9. psalm   I. Danish money

___ 10. Ingeborg   J. Capital of Denmark

___ handkerchief   K. Annemarie delivered to Uncle Henrik

___ Peter   L. Smuggled Jews out of Denmark

___ Sweden   M. All of Denmark is King Christian's

___ seasick   N. Contains words: It is he who numbers the stars one by one

___ bodyguard   O. Nazi symbol

II. Short Answer
 1. What is the Resistance?

Number the Stars Short Answer Unit Test 2 Page 2

2. What discovery did the girls make when they stopped at the button shop on their way home from school?

3. What caused the Rosens to change their plans to celebrate the Jewish New Year?

4. How do the Johansens help the Rosens that day?

5. How does Ellen verbally express the sadness she felt when Annemarie's older sister Lise died?

6. In what manner does the officer treat the baby photograph of Lise?

7. When her father calls Uncle Henrik, he uses two phrases that confuse Annemarie. What are they?

8. While looking at the sea, what information does Ellen share with Annemarie?

9. What rationed item does Annemarie joke about?

Number the Stars Short Answer Unit Test 2 Page 3

10. The girls are told about an event that will take place there that night. What is it? Whom is it for?

11. Tell what Annemarie is thinking while Peter reads the psalm.

12. What is really in the casket?

13. What does Peter give to Mr. Rosen and what are his instructions to him?

14. What does Annemarie find while examining her mother's ankle?

15. Whom does Annemarie will herself to act like when the soldiers stop her on the path?

16. How do the fishermen smuggle the Jews out of Denmark to Sweden?

17. In what way does Uncle Henrik say Annemarie helped the Jews?

Number the Stars Short Answer Unit Test 2 Page 4

18. What does Annemarie retrieve from Lise's trunk and what does she ask her father?

19. Tell the truth about Lise's death.

20. What does the young man, the author formed Peter's character from, wish for in his letter?

III. Quotations: Identify the speaker and explain the significance of these quotes:

1. "Yes, It is true. Any Danish citizen would die for King Christian, to protect him."

2. "It is their way of tormenting. For some reason, they want to torment Jewish people. It has happened in other countries. They have taken their time here- have let us relax alittle. But now it seems to be starting."

3. "Well, now I think that all of Denmark must be bodyguard for the Jews, as well."

4. "Don't be frightened, once I had three daughters. Tonight I am proud to have three daughters again."

Number the Stars Short Answer Unit Test 2 Page 5

5. "I remember it was raining, it was still raining the next morning when Mama told me. Mama was crying, and the rain made it seem as if the whole *world* was crying."

6. "I can't get it open! I never take it off- I can't even remember how to open it!"

7. "So, Henrik, is the weather good for fishing?"

8. "Run ahead and tell the house we've brought a friend."

9. "Tomorrow will be a day for fishing."

10. "But, it is much *easier* to be brave if you do not know everything. And so your Mama does not know everything. Neither do I. We know only what we need to know."

11. "Don't! That's Uncle Henrik's bread! My mother baked it!"

Number the Stars Short Answer Unit Test 2 Page 6

12. "Go on to your uncle and tell him the German dogs enjoyed his bread."

13. "And they have created a special drug. I don't know what it is, but it was in the handkerchief. It attracts the dogs, but when they sniff at it, it ruins their sense of smell. Imagine that!"

14. "You will, little one. You saved her life, after all. Someday you will find her again. Someday the war will end, all wars do."

Number the Stars Short Answer Unit Test 2 Page 7

IV. Vocabulary

Listen to the vocabulary word and spell it. After you have spelled all the words, go back and write down the definitions.

1.

2.

3.

4.

5.

6.

7.

8.

9.

10.

KEY: SHORT ANSWER UNIT TESTS - *Number the Stars*

The short answer questions are taken directly from the study guides.
If you need to look up the answers, you will find them in the study guide section.

Answers to the composition questions will vary depending on your
class discussions and the level of your students.

For the vocabulary section of the test, choose ten of the
words from the vocabulary lists to read orally for your students.

The answers to the matching section of the test are below.

Answers to the matching section of the Advanced Short Answer Unit Test
are the same as for Short Answer Unit Test #2.

Test #1	Test #2
1. B	1. I
2. G	2. H
3. E	3. J
4. J	4. C
5. L	5. G
6. N	6. O
7. C	7. E
8. H	8. A
9. O	9. N
10. D	10. L
11. I	11. K
12. A	12. B
13. K	13. D
14. F	14. F
15. M	15. M

ADVANCED SHORT ANSWER UNIT TEST - *Number the Stars*

I. Matching

___ 1. Resistance   A. Nazi symbol

___ 2. Christian X   B. Works secretly against Nazis

___ 3. Peter   C. Danish money

___ 4. Great Aunt Birte   D. Smuggled Jews out of Denmark

___ 5. Sweden   E. Red-headed fiance of Lise

___ 6. Copenhagen   F. How Mrs. Rosen felt in the boat

___ 7. kroner   G. Danish king

___ 8. typhus   H. Great Aunt Birte's cause of death

___ 9. handkerchief   I. Contains words: It is he who numbers the stars one by one

___ 10. Ingeborg   J. Pretend dead aunt

___ 11. psalm   K. Coast of Denmark near Sweden

___ 12. swastika   L. Jews were taken here by boat

___ 13. Gilleleje   M. All of Denmark is King Christian's

___ 14. seasick   N. Capital of Denmark

___ 15. bodyguard   O. Delivered to Uncle Henrik by Annemarie

II. Short Answer

1. What are the main conflicts in *Number the Stars* and how are they resolved?

Number the Stars Advanced Short Answer Unit Test Page 2

2. Annemarie finds out at the end of the story that Peter was in the Resistance. What earlier clues (foreshadowing) were there that Peter was a part of the Resistance?

3. Why does Mama offer to open the casket when she knows exactly what is inside?

4. Contrast Peter's behavior and personality *before* and *after* Lise's death.

5. For what reason did the author introduce the death of Annemarie's older sister into the plot?

6. Why did the Nazi soldier slap Mama?

7. While taking the basket to Uncle Henrik, Annemarie tells herself the story of "Little Red Riding Hood". Why did she do that?

8. What universal themes are present in *Number the Stars*?

Number the Stars Advanced Short Answer Unit Test Page 3

III. Essay
   Explain your definition of bravery, giving specific examples from the story to support it.

IV. Vocabulary
   Listen to the vocabulary words and write them down. After you have written down all the words, write a paragraph in which you use all the words. The paragraph must in some way relate to *Number the Stars*.

MULTIPLE CHOICE UNIT TEST 1 - *Number the Stars*

I. Matching

1. Resistance
2. Christian X
3. Peter
4. Great Aunt Birte
5. Sweden
6. Copenhagen
7. kroner
8. typhus
9. handkerchief
10. Ingeborg
11. psalm
12. swastika
13. Gilleleje
14. seasick
15. bodyguard

A. Nazi symbol
B. Works secretly against Nazis
C. Danish money
D. Smuggled Jews out of Denmark
E. Red-headed fiance of Lise
F. How Mrs. Rosen felt in the boat
G. Danish king
H. Great Aunt Birte's cause of death
I. Contains words: It is he who numbers the stars one by one
J. Pretend dead aunt
K. Coast of Denmark near Sweden
L. Jews were taken here by boat
M. All of Denmark is King Christian's
N. Capital of Denmark
O. Annemarie delivered to Uncle Henrik

II. Multiple Choice

1. Nazi occupation is
   a. when the Germans offered jobs.
   b. when the Nazis took over the country.
   c. when Hitler occupied Germany.
   d. when Sweden surrendered.

2. The Resistance is
   a. a secret group against the Nazis.
   b. the prevention of harm.
   c. an intense exercise.
   d. a Jewish group.

Number the Stars Multiple Choice Unit Test 1 Page 2

3. King Christian X's bodyguard is
    a. his son.
    b. the men of Copenhagen.
    c. all of Denmark.
    d. a fierce warrior.

4. King Christian X surrendered to Hitler because
    a. he knew too many Danish lives would be lost.
    b. Hitler threatened him.
    c. he was too old to fight.
    d. he thought it was too much work.

5. It was frightening for Annemarie to see Peter late at night because
    a. she was awakened from a nightmare.
    b. he was out past the curfew.
    c. he seemed very angry and upset.
    d. he had been drinking beer.

6. What Kirsti thought were fireworks really were
    a. thunderbolts.
    b. the Nazi soldiers practicing shooting from tanks.
    c. the Danish people blowing up their own naval fleet.
    d. her imagination.

7. Relocation means
    a. the Jews stay with their relatives for awhile.
    b. arresting the Resistance fighters.
    c. taking the Danes to Sweden.
    d. arresting the Jews and taking them away to camps and ghettos.

8. How does Ellen express how she feels about Lise's death?
    a. She wishes she wouldn't have died.
    b. She felt like the whole world was crying.
    c. She felt like crying all day.
    d. She wanted to change what had happened.

9. Annemarie yanks
    a. Ellen's pigtails.
    b. her covers over her head.
    c. Ellen's Star of David necklace.
    d. Kirsti's doll from her.

Number the Stars Multiple Choice Unit Test 1 Page 3

10. Mrs. Johansen thinks her husband should stay home from the trip because
    a. he needs the money and can't miss work.
    b. she wants a little vacation away from him and the house.
    c. it will look less suspicious.
    d. the kids will get on his nerves.

11. Mama warns the girls about
    a. the fishing village.
    b. the Nazis.
    c. talking to anyone.
    d. the dangers of the sea.

12. Annemarie is angry and confused because
    a. she is homesick.
    b. she has never heard of Great Aunt Birte.
    c. she wants to go to bed.
    d. she can't share a room with Ellen.

13. Uncle Henrik admits he and Mama lied to Annemarie because
    a. they couldn't trust her immaturity.
    b. they wanted to protect her.
    c. they were afraid.
    d. all of the above

14. As Peter reads the psalm aloud, Annemarie thinks
    a. about how scared she is.
    b. and wonders how someone could number each star because of the size of the sky.
    c. and wonders what will happen next.
    d. she will faint from exhaustion.

15. What quality does Annemarie see in the Jewish people as they leave?
    a. fear
    b. pride
    c. love
    d. freedom

16. While helping her mother, Annemarie finds
    a. the important packet Peter gave Mr. Rosen.
    b. the baby's medicine.
    c. the Bible from which Peter read.
    d. a secret place under the step.

Number the Stars Multiple Choice Unit Test 1 Page 4

17. When Annemarie reached the harbor, what was missing?
    a. the Jewish people
    b. the handkerchief
    c. the lunch basket
    d. her uncle's boat

18. Annemarie doesn't feel like she was brave because
    a. she was frightened.
    b. she didn't stand up to the Nazis.
    c. she is just an ordinary girl.
    d. she pretended to be her sister.

19. The handkerchief was important because
    a. it was a family heirloom .
    b. it had blood on it.
    c. it prevented the dogs from locating the scent of the Jews.
    d. it has Henrik's initials on it.

20. What news do the Johansen's hear of Peter?
    a. He is awarded a purple heart.
    b. He married another girl from Sweden.
    c. He moved to Sweden.
    d. He was executed by the Germans.

Number the Stars Multiple Choice Unit Test 1 Page 5

III. Quotations: Identify the speaker:

A= Annemarie   B= Ellen   C= Peter   D= Mr. Johansen   E= Mrs. Johansen
F= Kirsti   G= Nazis   H= Uncle Henrik

1. "Yes, It is true. Any Danish citizen would die for King Christian, to protect him."

2. "It is their way of tormenting. For some reason, they want to torment Jewish people. It has happened in other countries. They have taken their time here. But now it seems to be starting."

3. "Well, now I think that all of Denmark must be bodyguard for the Jews, as well."

4. "It was my birthday. I woke up in the night and I could hear the booms. And there were lights in the sky. Mama said it was fireworks for my birthday!"

5. "Don't be frightened, once I had three daughters. Tonight I am proud to have three daughters again."

6. "My father wants me to be teacher. He wants *everyone* to be a teacher, like him. But maybe I can convince him that I should go to acting school."

7. "I can't get it open! I never take it off- I can't even remember how to open it!"

8. "Where did you get the dark-haired one? From a different father? From the milkman?"

9. "If only I go with the girls, it will be safer. They are unlikely to suspect a woman and her children."

10. "And I have named him Thor, for the God of Thunder."

11. "Tomorrow will be a day for fishing."

12. "And they have created a special drug. I don't know what it is, but it was in the handkerchief. It attracts the dogs, but when they sniff at it, it ruins their sense of smell. Imagine that!"

Number the Stars Multiple Choice Unit Test 1 Page 6

IV. Vocabulary (Matching)

1. defiantly
2. obstinate
3. sabotage
4. intricate
5. disdainfully
6. designated
7. dubiously
8. imperious
9. synagogue
10. tentatively
11. deftly
12. staccato
13. condescending
14. commotion
15. latticed
16. tantalize
17. implored
18. insolently
19. deprivation
20. prejudiced

A. uncertainly; unsurely
B. assigned
C. stubborn
D. disturbance
E. detailed
F. biased; intolerant
G. Criss-crossed
H. domineering; overbearing
I. vandalize
J. skillfully
K. scornfully
L. tease; arouse
M. Jewish place of worship
N. doubtfully
O. superior
P. sharp abrupt sounds
Q. rudely; disrespectfully
R. pleaded; begged
S. boldly; rebelliously
T. hardship; need

MULTIPLE CHOICE UNIT TEST 2 - *Number the Stars*

I. Matching

1. kroner
2. typhus
3. Copenhagen
4. Great Aunt Birte
5. Gilleleje
6. swastika
7. Resistance
8. Christian X
9. psalm
10. Ingeborg
11. handkerchief
12. Peter
13. Sweden
14. seasick
15. bodyguard

A. Danish king
B. Red-headed fiance of Lise
C. Pretend dead aunt
D. Jews were taken here by boat
E. Works secretly against Nazis
F. How Mrs. Rosen felt in the boat
G. Coast of Denmark near Sweden
H. Great Aunt Birte's cause of death
I. Danish money
J. Capital of Denmark
K. Annemarie delivered to Uncle Henrik
L. Smuggled Jews out of Denmark
M. All of Denmark is King Christian's
N. Contains words: It is he who numbers the stars one by one
O. Nazi symbol

II. Multiple Choice

1. Members of the Resistance
    a. blew up ships.
    b. bombed railroads.
    c. smuggled Jews out.
    d. all of the above

2. On the way home from school, the girls discovered
    a. the button shop was closed.
    b. the soldiers were gone.
    c. the synagogue's glass was shattered.
    d. Kirsti was missing.

Number the Stars Multiple Choice Unit Test 2 Page 2

3. The Rosens did not celebrate the Jewish New Year due to
    a. the synagogue's list being taken by the Germans.
    b. their chicken getting burnt in the stove.
    c. their relatives visiting at the last minute.
    d. the Nazis harassing them.

4. The Johansens help the Rosens by
    a. cooking their chicken for them and saving it.
    b. hiding Ellen and helping the parents escape.
    c. giving them money.
    d. sending Ellen away to their relatives.

5. How does Ellen express how she feels about Lise's death?
    a. She wishes she wouldn't have died.
    b. She felt like the whole world was crying.
    c. She felt like crying all day.
    d. She wanted to change what had happened.

6. The officer treats Lise's baby photo
    a. carefully.
    b. carelessly.
    c. gently.
    d. destructively.

7. Choose the phrase that means something other than what it states.
    a. The eggs are fried.
    b. She will bring a carton of cigarettes.
    c. Is the weather good for fishing?
    d. Both b and c

8. Ellen shares with Annemarie that
    a. she is afraid of the sea.
    b. her father loves the sea.
    c. she used to visit the sea every summer.
    d. her mother is afraid of the sea.

9. Annemarie jokes about the rationed
    a. electricity.
    b. coffee.
    c. sugar.
    d. butter.

Number the Stars Multiple Choice Unit Test 2 Page 3

10. That night at Uncle Henrik's there will be
    a. a funeral.
    b. a dinner.
    c. a party.
    d. a seance.

11. As Peter reads the psalm aloud, Annemarie thinks
    a. about how scared she is.
    b. and wonders how someone could number each star because of the size of the sky.
    c. and wonders what will happen next.
    d. God is all-powerful.

12. In the casket are
    a. clothes and blankets.
    b. dead bodies they borrowed.
    c. lanterns and candles.
    d. guns and ammunition.

13. Peter's instructions to Mr. Rosen include to
    a. deliver the packet to Henrik without fail.
    b. deliver the envelope to the Swedish police.
    c. take the packet to the pretend funeral.
    d. wrap the lunch up in the basket to hide the packet.

14. While helping her mother, Annemarie finds
    a. the important packet Peter gave Mr. Rosen.
    b. the baby's medicine.
    c. the Bible from which Peter read.
    d. a secret place under the step.

15. When the soldiers stop her, Annemarie wills herself to act like
    a. Mama.
    b. Peter.
    c. Kirsti.
    d. Ellen.

16. The fishermen aided the Jews by
    a. finding their relatives for them.
    b. smuggling them in their boats to Sweden.
    c. feeding and clothing them.
    d. holding funerals for their friends.

Number the Stars Multiple Choice Unit Test 2 Page 4

17. Uncle Henrik admires Annemarie for
    a. milking Blossom.
    b. risking her life.
    c. taking the dark path.
    d. saving Ellen's necklace.

18. Annemarie learned that her sister Lise had been
    a. killed by the Nazis.
    b. run down by a car.
    c. a member of the Resistance.
    d. all of the above

19. Out of the Lise's trunk, Annemarie retrieves
    a. her Bible.
    b. the embroidered pillow.
    c. Ellen's necklace.
    d. Lise's yellow dress.

20. Annemarie asks her father
    a. why so many people had to die.
    b. to fix the necklace.
    c. what the psalm from the Bible meant.
    d. how many others are in the Resistance.

Number the Stars Multiple Choice Unit Test 2 page 5

III. Quotations: Identify the speaker:

A= Mr. Johansen   B= Nazis   C= Uncle Henrik   D= Annemarie   E=Peter
F= Ellen   G= Mrs. Johansen   H= Kirsti

1. "Yes, It is true. Any Danish citizen would die for King Christian, to protect him."

2. "It is their way of tormenting. For some reason, they want to torment Jewish people. It has happened in other countries. They have taken their time here. But now it seems to be starting."

3. "Well, now I think that all of Denmark must be bodyguard for the Jews, as well."

4. "It was my birthday. I woke up in the night and I could hear the booms. And there were lights in the sky. Mama said it was fireworks for my birthday!"

5. "Don't be frightened, once I had three daughters. Tonight I am proud to have three daughters again."

6. "My father wants me to be teacher. He wants *everyone* to be a teacher, like him. But maybe I can convince him that I should go to acting school."

7. "I can't get it open! I never take it off- I can't even remember how to open it!"

8. "Where did you get the dark-haired one? From a different father? From the milkman?"

9. "If only I go with the girls, it will be safer. They are unlikely to suspect a woman and her children."

10. "And I have named him Thor, for the God of Thunder."

11. "Tomorrow will be a day for fishing."

12. "And they have created a special drug. I don't know what it is, but it was in the handkerchief. It attracts the dogs, but when they sniff at it, it ruins their sense of smell. Imagine that!"

Number the Stars Multiple Choice Unit Test 2 page 6

IV. Vocabulary (Matching)

1. defiantly   A. detailed

2. obstinate   B. assigned

3. sabotage   C. skillfully

4. intricate   D. disturbance

5. disdainfully   E. uncertainly; unsurely

6. designated   F. doubtfully

7. dubiously   G. sharp abrupt sounds

8. imperious   H. domineering; overbearing

9. synagogue   I. superior

10. tentatively   J. stubborn

11. deftly   K. biased; intolerant

12. staccato   L. scornfully

13. condescending   M. vandalize

14. commotion   N. rudely; disrespectfully

15. latticed   O. Jewish place of worship

16. tantalize   P. hardship; need

17. implored   Q. tease; arouse

18. insolently   R. pleaded; begged

19. deprivation   S. boldly; rebelliously

20. prejudiced   T. criss-crossed

ANSWER SHEET - *Number the Stars*
Multiple Choice Unit Tests

I. Matching	II. Multiple Choice	III. Quotes	IV. Vocabulary
1. ___	1. ___	1. ___	1. ___
2. ___	2. ___	2. ___	2. ___
3. ___	3. ___	3. ___	3. ___
4. ___	4. ___	4. ___	4. ___
5. ___	5. ___	5. ___	5. ___
6. ___	6. ___	6. ___	6. ___
7. ___	7. ___	7. ___	7. ___
8. ___	8. ___	8. ___	8. ___
9. ___	9. ___	9. ___	9. ___
10. ___	10. ___	10. ___	10. ___
11. ___	11. ___	11. ___	11. ___
12. ___	12. ___	12. ___	12. ___
13. ___	13. ___		13. ___
14. ___	14. ___		14. ___
15. ___	15. ___		15. ___
	16. ___		16. ___
	17. ___		17. ___
	18. ___		18. ___
	19. ___		19. ___
	20. ___		20. ___

ANSWER KEY MULTIPLE CHOICE UNIT TESTS – *Number the Stars*

Answers to Unit Test 1 are in the left column. Answers to Unit Test 2 are in the right column.

I. Matching	II. Multiple Choice	III. Quotes	IV. Vocabulary
1. B I	1. B D	1. D A	1. S S
2. G H	2. A A	2. C E	2. C J
3. E J	3. C A	3. A D	3. I M
4. J C	4. B B	4. F H	4. E A
5. L G	5. B B	5. D A	5. K L
6. N O	6. C D	6. B F	6. B B
7. C E	7. D D	7. A F	7. N F
8. H A	8. B D	8. G B	8. H H
9. O N	9. C A	9. E G	9. M O
10. D L	10. C A	10. F H	10. A E
11. I K	11. C B	11. H C	11. J C
12. A B	12. B A	12. H C	12. P G
13. K D	13. B A		13. O I
14. F F	14. B A		14. D D
15. M M	15. B C		15. G T
	16. A B		16. L Q
	17. A B		17. R R
	18. A D		18. Q N
	19. C B		19. T P
	20. D C		20. F K

UNIT RESOURCE MATERIALS

BULLETIN BOARD IDEAS - *Number the Stars*

1. Save a space for students' best writing. Make a nice border. Maybe something from the novel like Stars of David or stars in a starry night. Cut out the letters SHINING STARS or something else to designate quality work. Staple up the best writing samples (or quizzes or whatever you have graded) on colorful paper.

2. Bring in (or have students bring in) pictures of Denmark, Copenhagen, the North and Baltic Seas, castles, kings, fishing harbors, etc. Make a collage if you have enough different pictures (or post individual pictures on colorful paper if you only have a few pictures). This could also be a fun introductory activity for students to create a quick bulletin board.

3. Draw one of the word search puzzles onto the bulletin board. (Be sure to enlarge it.) Write the key words to one side. Invite students to take their pens or markers and find the words before and/or after class (or perhaps this could be an activity for students who finish their work early).

4. Have artistic students create a mural depicting Copenhagen, Denmark, Europe, the harbor at Gilleleje, Uncle Henrik's house, King Christian's palace at Amalienborg, etc. Less artistic, but interested students, could do the research to give to the artists for authenticity.

5. Students could create poems using the outline of the Star of David for the basis. They could include words and phrases associated with their concept of this symbol. These could be posted for display.

6. Duplicate the actual words to the entire psalm (Psalm 147) Peter read aloud from the Bible the night the Nazis came to Uncle Henrik's. Have students illustrate their impression of the meaning of the words and lines.

7. Compare life in Denmark during World War II with your students' lives. Have them come up with a list of major differences, advantages, disadvantages, etc. Have them illustrate the differences and display in a creative manner.

8. Artistic students could illustrate some of the tactics the Resistance members used to deter the Nazis. For example, the blowing up of the Danish naval fleet, or the smuggling of the Jews to Sweden.

9. Review on a map the route the girls and Mama took by train from Copenhagen to Uncle Henrik's by the sea. Reread that section for details to help you locate the exact way they traveled. Create a large scale impression of their trip, including places they saw along the way.

10. Portray the main characters and display surrounded with appropriate items that demonstrate their individuality.

EXTRA ACTIVITIES - *Number the Stars*

One of the difficulties in teaching a novel is that all students don't read at the same speed. One student who likes to read may take the book home and finish it in a day or two. Sometimes a few students finish the in-class assignments early. The problem, then, is finding suitable extra activities for students.

The best thing I've found is to keep a little library in the classroom. For this unit on *Number the Stars*, you might check out from the school library other books by Lois Lowry. A biography of the author would be interesting for some students. You may include other related books and articles about: World War II, Denmark, Sweden, the Jewish religion and practices, rationing, Resistance movements in other European countries, other W.W. II escape stories, underground newspapers, concentration camps, ghettos, etc.

Other things you may keep on hand are puzzles. We have made some relating directly to *Number the Stars* for you. Feel free to duplicate them.

Some students may like to draw. You might devise a contest or allow some extra-credit grade for students who draw characters or scenes from *Number the Stars*. Note, too, that if the students do not want to keep their drawings you may pick up some extra bulletin board materials this way. If you have a contest and you supply the prize or, you could possibly make the drawing itself a non-refundable entry fee.

The pages which follow contain games, puzzles and worksheets. The keys, when appropriate, immediately follow the puzzle or worksheet. There are two main groups of activities: one group for the unit; that is, generally relating to the *Number the Stars* text, and another group of activities related strictly to the *Number the Stars* vocabulary.

Directions for the games, puzzles and worksheets are self-explanatory. The object here is to provide you with extra materials you may use in any way you choose.

MORE ACTIVITIES - *Number the Stars*

1. Pick a chapter or scene with a great deal of dialogue and have the students act it out on a stage. (Perhaps you could assign various scenes to different groups of students so more than one scene could be acted and more students could participate.)

2. The Danish Resistance produced an underground newspaper to spread information about their cause. Have a group of interested students create a newspaper supporting some viable social issue.

3. Have students design a book cover (front and back and inside flaps) for *Number the Stars*.

4. Research more thoroughly the rationing needed during the war. Create a menu listing alternative and available foods in place of regular fare. Illustrate your selections.

5. Students could have a footrace, like Annemarie was conditioning herself to be ready for at school. They could design ribbons that reflect something from the story.

6. Use some of the related topics (noted earlier for an in-class library) as topics for research, reports or written papers, or as topics for guest speakers.

7. Have students plan and teach a lesson on a chapter or section of the book. Give them guidelines and a time frame.

8. *Gone With the Wind* was Mama's favorite story. Perhaps a small group would like to read it or watch the movie, then report back to the class. They could dramatize some of it like the girls were doing in the book.

9. Discuss the tradition of trousseaus and do some research on it. Girls in your class may want to itemize what they would like to be in their trousseaus. They could make a trunk, like what was in Annemarie's corner, out of cardboard and put miniature or paper items in it to represent their trousseau.

10. Write to Lois Lowry asking her questions students have composed. You could send a class set of letters in one large envelope.

11. Do an experiment with the class on the amount of light needed to do homework. Mr. Rosen had to grade his papers by dim candlelight. Try doing homework by candlelight to see what it was like. Imagine having only candlelight nightly for *years*. Would the seasons affect the amount of light available in the evenings in Scandinavia? Report your findings to the class.

More Activities - *Number the Stars* Page 2

12. Show some films that have similar settings or themes such as: Disney Channel's *Friendship in Vienna*, or ColumbiaTriStar's *Alan and Naomi*. Both of these movies display courageous young people helping their Jewish counterparts during this time period. Students could watch them and then compare them to *Number the Stars*.

13. Allow students to select a character from the novel. Have them dress like them, speak like them; assume their persona. Create a talk show format with these characters as the guests. Have a student volunteer to be the host. Others not involved will be the audience, questioning the characters. Have a topic like: courage, loyalty, risking your life for another, etc. - themes encountered in the novel. Allow the class to decide as much as possible. Have questions from the audience ready prior to the show day. You could have students try out for the parts. Remind them to keep it on the up and up, not to mimic some of the seedier talk shows. This will require students to take an in-depth look into the characterization in the novel.

14. Due to the shortage of leather, Kirsti had to have shoes made of fish scales. Create alternatives for those items usually made of leather like: shoes, purses, belts, etc. Explain how they could be made and with what material to hold up similarly to leather. Illustrate your creations.

15. If feasible, take the class to a memorial or museum honoring victims of the Holocaust such as the National Holocaust Museum in Washington D. C.

16. Encourage students to read some other timely pieces such as: *Diary of a Young Girl, The Upstairs Room, Friedrich, Briar Rose, Stepping on the Cracks, Rose Blanche*, etc.

17. Students who like board games may want to create one using information from this novel. Some students could work together as a group to complete this task. Encourage them to look at setting to illustrate their board and possibly use vocabulary, characters, plot, etc. for question cards.

18. Crocheting is one of Mama's hobbies and she creates lovely things. Demonstrate this form of needlework (or have a skilled class member's parent or grandparent do it) and encourage interested students to learn how. Display any of their subsequent creations.

19. Have a favorite fairy tale session. Students could select their favorite one and read or tell to the class.

20. Bake together, if possible, a large number of pink frosted cupcakes and hold a celebration party honoring the Danish Jewish people's survival due to their courageous Danish friends.

More Activities - *Number the Stars* Page 3

21. Annemarie said it seemed like they ate potatoes every night. Look up and share a variety of potato recipes and perhaps students could prepare some of them at home and bring back to class to sample if time is a factor in preparing them in class.

22. Create a pretend forest and path like Annemarie had to travel on between her uncle's house and the harbor. Act that scene out using your set.

23. Codes were used to communicate between Uncle Henrik and the Johansens. Have a set of students devise their own code to communicate among themselves. Reward those outside the group who can break the code!

WORD SEARCH - *Number the Stars*

All the words in this list are associated with *Number the Stars*. The words are placed backwards, forward, diagonally, up and down. The included words are listed below the word search.

```
V S S D Y L D L P B J D H P N H F D E W D Q Q T
Z G N I T E H C O R C K R O N E R K R T R U N K
B L Z K N B S D F W Y H R U I G S U R R J E R M
E K V M V D Y I Q N R T R H N N C O T P L Q L W
X I A F R G S J L A H Y C I A K F D R L R A N L
G R R E U H C T W S E R Q D S A A T E R S I C Q
K I T A S N A U E V E S E A S T S R Y P M O D V
H E R H M G E A P K R I C T M U I J D P P D W E
P D O A E E S R D C R K W I A R S A U E H A N N
B E I T F I N N A F A N Z C T A S N N B N U L Q
S L T N C F A N E L E K O Z K L I H R X I C S S
G A O K G H E D A D H L E I Q F A E I X M L W S
K H Z S V E H W E Q O T T S F G H B Q R T D E N
N Q N D S W B W C H Q S Y O E T K K I R S T I E
X C V V P O S O X J A X C N A L J V P V P H R H
D W Z K C X M Q R W B K K E S P E C I A L C M M
F I R E W O R K S G Y E L L O W D R E S S D R W
```

ANNEMARIE	DRUNKARD	KIRSTI	RUCKSACK
BALTICSEA	ELLEN	KRONER	SEASICK
BLOSSOM	FIREWORKS	LEATHER	SLAPPED
BODYGUARD	FISHSHOES	LISE	SPECIAL
CHRISTIANX	FUNERAL	LOWRY	SWASTIKA
COFFIN	GIRAFFE	MRROSEN	SWEDEN
COPENHAGEN	HANDKERCHIEF	MRSHIRSH	TROFAST
CROCHETING	HOLOCAUST	NORTHSEA	TRUNK
CUPCAKES	INGEBORG	PETER	TYPHUS
DEFRIEDANSKE	JUBILEE	PRIDE	
DENMARK	KATTEGAT	PSALM	
YELLOWDRESS			

CROSSWORD - *Number the Stars*

CROSSWORD CLUES - *Number the Stars*

ACROSS
1. Used to prevent Ellen's detection
5. Once you're greeted by a king
7. Cause of Great Aunt Birte's death
8. None is available during war
10. Fatihful dog of Mama's
14. Danish money
15. Older sister of Annemarie and Kirsti
17. Ingest food
21. Pretend dead aunt
25. Belonging to him
26. Strong Jewish trait
27. Finished
28. Negative reply
29. Kirsti refused to wear
30. Obstinate younger sister of Annemarie

DOWN
1. Red-headed fiance of Lise
2. Petrol; fuel
3. Courageous young Danish girl
4. Persecution of Jews by Nazis
5. Nazi symbol
6. Author
9. Jewish friend of Annemarie
10. Copenhagen fun spot
11. Lise's trousseau is in it
12. Mrs. Johansen did this the night Lise was killed
13. Danish fairy tale author
16. Jews were taken to this place by boat
18. Borders Denmark to the east
19. Button shop lady
20. How Mrs. Rosen felt in the boat
22. Borders Denmark to the west
23. Provided family with milk
24. Pink frosted ones were nowhere to be found

CROSSWORD ANSWER KEY - *Number the Stars*

MATCHING QUIZ/WORKSHEET 1 - *Number the Stars*

___ 1. Bodyguard   A. Annemarie's Jewish friend

___ 2. De Frie Danske   B. Royalty-carrying white horse

___ 3. Ellen   C. Mama's favorite story

___ 4. Cupcakes   D. Girls' bookbag

___ 5. Fireworks   E. Lise danced in it on engagement

___ 6. Giraffe   F. Provided milk

___ 7. Rucksack   G. Explosions of naval fleet on Kirsti's birthday

___ 8. Lise   H. None available during war

___ 9. Jubilee   I. Kirsti's kitten

___ 10. Trunk   J. All of Denmark is King Christian's

___ 11. Kroner   K. Author

___ 12. Osterbrogade   L. Danish money

___ 13. Gone With The Wind   M. The Free Danes (underground newspaper)

___ 14. Lowry   N. Annemarie's older deceased sister

___ 15. Mrs. Hirsh   O. Trick to fool Nazi soldiers

___ 16. Yellow dress   P. Copenhagen street

___ 17. Blossom   Q. Button shop lady

___ 18. Funeral   R. Pink frosted ones are unavailable

___ 19. Leather   S. Holds Lise's trousseau

___ 20. God of Thunder   T. Nickname for tall Nazi soldier

MATCHING QUIZ/WORKSHEET 2 - *Number the Stars*

___ 1. Star of David   A. Capital of Denmark

___ 2. Trofast   B. Worked against Nazis

___ 3. Swastika   C. Danish king

___ 4. Coffin   D. Annemarie delivered to Uncle Henrik

___ 5. Uncle Henrik   E. Fisherman who lives by the sea

___ 6. Photograph   F. Red-headed fiance of Lise

___ 7. Christian   G. Kirsti refused to wear

___ 8. Typhus   H. Used to prevent Ellen's detection

___ 9. Kattegat   I. Once you are greeted by a king

___10. Slapped   J. Strong Jewish trait

___11. Resistance   K. Annemarie often told Kirsti

___12. Handkerchief   L. Smuggled Jews out of Denmark

___13. Fish Shoes   M. Hid clothes and blankets

___14. Pride   N. Symbol of Jewish faith

___15. Little Red Riding Hood   O. Mrs. Rosen's feeling in boat

___16. Copenhagen   P. Mama's faithful dog

___17. Special   Q. Nazi symbol

___18. Seasick   R. Soldier did this to Mama

___19. Ingeborg   S. Great Aunt's cause of death

___20. Peter   T. Channel of the North Sea near Sweden

KEY: MATCHING QUIZ/WORKSHEETS - *Number the Stars*

Worksheet 1	Worksheet 2
1. J	1. N
2. M	2. P
3. A	3. Q
4. R	4. M
5. G	5. E
6. T	6. H
7. D	7. C
8. N	8. S
9. B	9. T
10. S	10. R
11. L	11. B
12. P	12. D
13. C	13. G
14. K	14. J
15. Q	15. K
16. E	16. A
17. F	17. I
18. O	18. O
19. H	19. L
20. I	20. F

JUGGLE LETTER REVIEW GAME CLUE SHEET - *Number the Stars*

SCRAMBLED	WORD	CLUE
YPUSTH	TYPHUS	Cause of Great Aunt Birte's death
TRCCHGNIOE	CROCHETING	Mrs. Johansen did this the night Lise died
KISSCAE	SEASICK	How Mrs. Rosen felt in the boat
GGIEBORN	INGEBORG	Smuggled Jews out of Denmark
DDUAKNRR	DRUNKARD	What Mama looked like when she hurt her ankle
DEPIR	PRIDE	Strong Jewish trait
NOFICF	COFFIN	Hid clothes and blankets
MAPSL	PSALM	Contains: it is he who numbers the stars
GSARDBEEOOTR	OSTERBROGADE	Copenhagen street
ESSRANTEI	RESISTANCE	Worked against Nazis
RTNKU	TRUNK	Lise's trousseau is in it
REETP	PETER	Red-headed fiance of Lise
UCCKSEP	CUPCAKES	Pink frosted ones are unavailable
BLUEJIE	JUBILEE	Royalty-carrying white horse
RRWFKIEOS	FIREWORKS	What Kirsti thought explosion of naval fleet was
EENNAAIMR	ANNEMARIE	Courageous young Danish girl
ENLEL	ELLEN	Jewish friend of Annemarie
SKRTII	KIRSTI	Obstinate younger sister of Annemarie
RIFEGAF	GIRAFFE	Nickname for tall Nazi soldier
GOBDDRUAGY	BODYGUARD	All of Denmark is King Christian's
AAKTGTTE	KATTEGAT	Channel of the North Sea near Sweden
LAICEPS	SPECIAL	What you are if greeted by a king
AKSITAWS	SWATISKA	Nazi symbol
DEPAPLS	SLAPPED	What Nazi soldier did to Mama
REHTAEL	LEATHER	None was available during war
TSAFORT	TROFAST	Mama's faithful dog
OOSMSLB	BLOSSOM	Provided family with milk
EEELLLJIG	GILLELEJE	Coast of Denmark near Sweden
FEEIHRCDKNAH	HANDKERCHIEF	Annemarie delivered to Uncle Henrik
HHPPOOARGT	PHOTOGRAPH	Used to prevent Ellen's detection
MNKDREA	DENMARK	Setting
ARELNFU	FUNERAL	Trick to fool Nazis
OAESNHTR	NORTHSEA	Borders Denmark to the west
AIXCNRHTS	CHRISTIANX	Danish king
ILES	LISE	Older sister of Kirsti and Annemarie
RRMENSO	MRROSEN	Jewish schoolteacher
KKCCUARS	RUCKSACK	Girls' bookbag
FEEEIARDDKSN	DEFRIEDANSKE	The Free Danes (underground newspaper)
WYLOR	LOWRY	Author
RREONK	KRONER	Danish money

VOCABULARY RESOURCE MATERIALS

VOCABULARY WORD SEARCH - *Number the Stars*

All the words in this list are associated with *Number the Stars* with emphasis on the vocabulary words being studied in the unit. The words are placed backwards, forward, diagonally, up and down. The included words are listed below the word search.

```
I M P A S S I V E Q N D Y T N S T T P K L D M W
I Y L N N A S S E B K V J L Y J R F W J K L M N
G M L Y J L B T V S B M Z N S U J L W K W H F K
K C P L K D A B X Y Y X A J D U Y J V G O Q Y Y
U Y T R A N B S A X G G I G W F O H N O M T Y L
I N T R I C A T E T O Y E M B R O I D E R E D F
H K W T A N I L N G H D K D P Z T L B O X E R J
S A S A G B T T U K A H E Z W E U I U U T H B D
C B U S V W B E S P K T M W H M R S N A D D H Y
O O T G H E T I D A A W O C S H S I R T E K L V
B C N K H T R H L N C S O B C E M E O G O T M R
X M H T J T R I G D N R D W A P P G R U N N P P
C M G R E X I I N Y C R A U L S P E T A S Z E R
Q Z Z G X M S L J G H X T S A P M T I V N Q C D
J F D N Q E P M Y H K B S X M B N F M Q B N H P
H R F J D K F T R R D F E M U M E M N Y K H Q J
H V R W Y L L U F N I A D S I D L C L X J S M Z
```

EXASPERATED
HAUGHTILY
HOODLUMS
INTRICATE
IMPERIOUS
SABBATH
TROUSSEAU
RABBI
CROCHETING
SUBMERGED
INTONED
UNWAVERING
IMPASSIVE

DESIGNATED
DEFIANTLY
EMBROIDERED
CONTEMPT
DUBIOUSLY
SARCASTICALLY
SYNAGOGUE
LANKY
TRUDGED
IMPRINTED
DISDAINFULLY
OBSTINATE
SABOTAGE

VOCABULARY CROSSWORD - *Number the Stars*

VOCABULARY CROSSWORD CLUES - *Number the Stars*

ACROSS
1. In a hostile manner
8. Disgust; distaste
11. Obstinate younger sister of Annemarie
13. Jewish minister
15. Unhappy
16. Look
18. A single
19. Vandalize
20. Jews were taken to this place by boat
22. Domineering; overbearing
24. Negative reply
26. Strong Jewish trait
27. Opposite of young
28. North Sea channel between Sweden and Denmark
30. Area where homes are located
31. Author
32. Jewish friend of Annemarie
33. Definite article

DOWN
2. Decorated with needlework
3. Lean; thin
4. Annoyed; irritated
5. Items brought to marriage by bride
6. Recited; spoke
7. Unemotional; indifferent
9. Plodded; marched
10. Doubtfully
12. Needlework similar to knitting
14. Criminals; hooligans
17. Copenhagen street
21. Jewish schoolteacher
23. Holy day
25. Red-headed fiance of Lise
29. Older sister of Annemarie and Kirsti

VOCABULARY CROSSWORD ANSWER KEY - *Number the Stars*

VOCABULARY WORKSHEET 1 - *Number the Stars*

____ 1. Contempt   A. Uncertainly; unsurely

____ 2. Haughtily   B. Unchanging

____ 3. Tentatively   C. Holy day

____ 4. Distorted   D. Arrogantly; high and mightily

____ 5. Impassive   E. Disgust; distaste

____ 6. Disdainfully   F. Scornfully

____ 7. Lanky   G. Lean; thin

____ 8. Unwavering   H. Twisted; deformed

____ 9. Sophisticated   I. Stubborn

____ 10. Imperious   J. Cultured; refined

____ 11. Belligerently   K. Pressed into

____ 12. Imprinted   L. In a hostile manner

____ 13. Sabbath   M. Unemotional; indifferent

____ 14. Obstinate   N. Domineering; overbearing

____ 15. Dubiously   O. Strawlike

____ 16. Reluctantly   P. Doubtfully

____ 17. Massive   Q. Plodded; marched

____ 18. Wispy   R. Secured; held fast

____ 19. Anchored   S. Huge

____ 20. Trudged   T. Unwillingly; hesitantly

VOCABULARY WORKSHEET 2 - *Number the Stars*

____ 1. Scandinavian   A. Discovery

____ 2. Military   B. Shrunk back; flinched

____ 3. Gesturing   C. Entered; invaded

____ 4. Deftly   D. Sticking out

____ 5. Mourning   E. Disastrous; ruinous

____ 6. Surge   F. Motioning

____ 7. Condescending   G. Referring to northern European countries

____ 8. Extinguished   H. Offering

____ 9. Protruding   I. Superior

____ 10. Winced   J. Sudden forward movement

____ 11. Rummaging   K. Honor; decency

____ 12. Stricken   L. Put on

____ 13. Donned   M. Dreary; grim

____ 14. Lunged   N. Rush

____ 15. Devastating   O. Having to do with army or soldiers

____ 16. Bleak   P. Grieving

____ 17. Permeated   Q. Hit by strong emotion

____ 18. Integrity   R. Searching through

____ 19. Sacrifice   S. Put out

____ 20. Detection   T. Skillfully

KEY: VOCABULARY WORKSHEETS - *Number the Stars*

Worksheet 1	Worksheet 2
1. E	1. G
2. D	2. O
3. A	3. F
4. H	4. T
5. M	5. P
6. F	6. N
7. G	7. I
8. B	8. S
9. J	9. D
10. N	10. B
11. L	11. R
12. K	12. Q
13. C	13. L
14. I	14. J
15. P	15. E
16. T	16. M
17. S	17. C
18. O	18. K
19. R	19. H
20. Q	20. A

VOCABULARY JUGGLE LETTER REVIEW GAME CLUES - *Number the Stars*

SCRAMBLED	WORD	CLUE
LYHIALYTRHMC	RHYTHMICALLY	To a uniform beat
EEDDJIRCPU	PREJUDICED	Biased; intolerant
TYLDEF	DEFTLY	Skillfully
MEDETRPAT	PERMEATED	Entered; invaded
SEEARH	HEARSE	Funeral vehicle
OTTEECDNI	DETECTION	Discovery
NOUINGMR	MOURNING	Grieving
IINPEDRAVOT	DEPRIVATION	Hardship; need
UEYCNRG	URGENCY	Seriousness
TTRYIIGEN	INTEGRITY	Honor; decency
UERSG	SURGE	Rush
CCIIFERAS	SACRIFICE	Offering
AAOTTCCS	STACCATO	Sharp, abrupt sounds
KLABE	BLEAK	Dreary; grim
OEEICNDSCNDGN	CONDESCENDING	Superior
DEEAMLG	GLEAMED	Shone; flickered
EINUIXETGSHD	EXTINGUISHED	Put out
AAEIVGTTDNS	DEVASTATING	Disastrous; ruinous
UAIGGMMRN	RUMMAGING	Searching through
DDSSBUIE	SUBSIDED	Let up; eased
RRUOPDTGNI	PROTRUDING	Sticking out
NUDGEL	LUNGED	Sudden forward movement
MMOOOICTN	COMMOTION	Disturbance
USCCTIA	CAUSTIC	Harsh
CENWID	WINCED	Shrunk back; flinched
NONDDE	DONNED	Put on
ALKOC	CLOAK	Outer garment
UTTA	TAUT	Tight
ZAATTIENL	TANTALIZE	Tease; arouse
IENSRTKC	STRICKEN	Hit by strong emotion
LOSCD	SCOLD	Nag
KLANY	LANKY	Lean; thin
UNGRITSGE	GESTURING	Motioning
BARIB	RABBI	Jewish minister
PYSWI	WISPY	Straw-like
VAMSISE	MASSIVE	Huge
HABSTBA	SABBATH	Holy day
NNDEIOT	INTONED	Recited; spoke
GGSEUOANY	SYNAGOGUE	Jewish place of worship
TTDDEIORS	DISTORTED	Twisted; deformed